DARK PSYCHOLOGY

AND

MANIPULATION

How to Become A Master of Your Own Mind and Influence The Actions Of Others. Discover Time-Tested Mind Control and Hypnosis Techniques That Impacted Millions.

HAPPINESS FACTORY
Be Who you Want!

TEXT COPYRIGHT © HAPPINESS FACTORY

LEGAL & DISCLAIMER

TABLE OF CONTENTS

ABOUT HAPPINESS FACTORY

BRING HAPPINESS TO YOUR LIFE

Are you in control of your life?

Can you tell that your mind is under the control of another person? Do you know why you act the way you do and say the words that come out of your mind?

Perhaps you have a low or below-average IQ, and you feel you can never do well in your career.

Dark psychology and manipulation are real in our world today. Many people wake up in the morning and run through the day without any control over what they are doing. Who do you think is controlling them? Maybe you fall into this category. Happiness Factory is here to help.

We will help you bring peace, purpose, and stability to your professional and personal life. At Happiness Factory, we devise content for both men and women and help them understand and validate their problems and ultimately bring happiness to their lives. We all face hundreds of issues in our daily lives, but we can solve many of them with some alteration to our mindset and how we process emotions.

Experiencing happiness can fundamentally change how we think, act, and live our lives. Negative experiences can minimize or altogether eliminate joy from our life, and this is why our researchers provide insight into the best possible solutions to your problems. We want to make sure that you can live your life in the best possible way.

By reading our books, you will understand what goes on in your mind and how your body reacts to the different types of mental and emotional stress you face in your personal and professional life. From problems in your personal relationships to work-related stress, we at Happiness Factory will help you channel your inner strength to conquer any problem in any sphere of your life.

Learn how to live your best life with the help of the Happiness Factory Book Collection.

DARK PSYCHOLOGY

INTRODUCTION TO DARK PSYCHOLOGY

Dark Psychology is the human state's analysis regarding individuals' psychological character to prey upon other people. All of humankind can victimize other people and animals. Even though many control this trend, some act upon those instincts. Dark Psychology attempts to understand the ideas, emotions, and senses that result in human predatory behavior.

Dark Psychology presumes this production is purposeful and contains a proper, goal-oriented motivation 99.99% of the time. Under Dark Behavior, the residual .01% is that others' brutal exploitation with no purpose or reasonably characterized by literary science or spiritual dogma.

Dark Psychology claims there's a place within the individual mind that enables many people to commit horrific acts with no intention. It presupposes that all individuals possess a measure of malicious intent towards other people, ranging from minimally obtrusive and momentary ideas to pure psychopathic aberrant behaviors with no cohesive reasoning.

DARK PSYCHOLOGY DEFINED

"Dark Psychology" is both a human consciousness construct and study of the human condition as it relates to the psychological nature of people to prey upon others motivated by psychopathic, deviant or psychopathological criminal drives that lack purpose and general assumptions of instinctual drives, evolutionary biology, and social sciences theory. All of humanity has the potentiality to victimize humans and other living creatures. While many restrain or sublimate this tendency, some act upon these impulses. Dark Psychology explores criminal, deviant, and cybercriminal minds." Michael Nuccitelli, Psy.D. [2006]

Dark Psychology is the art and science of manipulation and mind control. While Psychology is the study of human behavior and is central to our thoughts, actions, and interactions, the term Dark Psychology is the phenomenon by which people use tactics of motivation, persuasion, manipulation, and coercion to get what they want.

Dark psychology is the science and art of manipulation and mind control. On its own, psychology is the study of how humans behave, the mind and the thoughts, and how we interact with each other.

Dark psychology is when people use maneuvers, motivations, manipulations, persuasion, and compulsion to achieve their goals.

IS DARK PSYCHOLOGY AND MANIPULATION REAL?

Everyone likes to believe they are in control of their mind and action. People rarely admit that someone else can control them.

Some cannot even fathom the idea of being controlled, while others can't understand the concept.

The study of Dark psychology and manipulation has revealed that humans are not often in control of their actions, but they think they are. For example, most people believe they have a steady self that has acted and behaved in a certain way over time. Hence, they are very sure they can predict how they will act under certain circumstances in the future. However, can you entirely be sure of how you react when you find yourself under extreme pressure? How about how you will respond when you are in crisis?

A lot of people would love to feel that, at an exigency, they would have the ability to remain calm, lead others, act courageously, or, above all, keep their beliefs. For instance, in a nonviolent situation. What about your ethical code? Are you going to be able to stay up for yourself or withstand the orders of an authority figure? Study shows that you may not have such control of yourself, words, and reaction as you always think you do.

Studies have shown that only a few people can predict how we will behave under intense stress. This is due to the concept of dark psychology and manipulation. When we are under pressure, most of us undergo a flight response that changes to help us survive potentially harmful experiences and, among other matters, shuts down a great deal of functioning when triggered.

This is a superb strategy for surviving an assault, but in a contemporary world, where we need our greater functioning when we are under pressure. In other words, once we encounter certain levels of anxiety or are at actual or suspected threat, we do not think clearly or act in the ways we had already thought we would.

[3]

SOME INTERESTING SCENARIOS

Let's start by looking at two controversial psychological experiments in the 1960s and '70s. The first experiment was carried out by a renowned researcher, Stanly Milgram, in his obedience study.

In this study, volunteers have been advised they would be engaging in a learning survey. They were seated in a panel using a speaker and microphone, and a dial. The participants were informed that an actor was in a different area, and they would be required to ask pre-scripted questions using the microphone and hearing the speaker's answer.

If the student gave the incorrect response, the volunteer would administer an electrical shock by placing the dial's voltage. The dial was tagged from moderate through to extraordinarily debilitating and lethal.

Participants were informed by the researcher, who had been wearing a white laboratory coat to keep on applying shocks at increasing intensity into the student,' even though they might hear the student was in pain, like mimicked screams of pain.

If the volunteer refused to proceed, he or she would be advised to carry on with the script as follows:

- Please continue.

- The experiment requires you to proceed.

- You must proceed.

- You don't have another option. You must proceed.

Here's the exciting part, even while suffering intense anxiety, 65% of volunteers applied the deadly' jolt. People who insisted that the experiment be stopped failed to ask to check about the student's health. The majority claimed they would not act this way, but could not resist the authority figure'.

In his submission, Milgram used his findings to explain the type of obedience Nazi soldiers carried out during World War 2.

In another experiment, this time by the American psychologist Philip Zimbardo. Also known as the Stanford Prison Experiment. Zimbardo reinforced the belief that people can be manipulated into doing things they do not intend to do, especially in a difficult way.

In this experiment, a group of students agreed to a prison simulation. A cellar in the university was altered to resemble a prison, with as much precision as you can imagine. The participants were randomly assigned to the part of prisoner or guard.

Initially intended to operate for fourteen days, the experiment was closed down after only six days due to the prison guards' disturbing behavior. They started without prompting, to act in savage ways toward the 'offenders.'

Much like the Milgram study, participants thought they would behave 'morally.' They intended to act naturally before the experiment kicked off, but they found themselves behaving in highly unpredictable and disagreeable manners in a relatively short time frame.

Other experiments have shown that we will concur with a team, though we know that our opinion or position was right while they are incorrect. We would instead slack when we are in a group or team because we could get away with it without being held responsible (social loafing). We would frequently act out of character within a bunch and be readily manipulated into altering our view when specific conditions are indicated like authority, security, or relaxation.

The most peculiar thing about this study is not merely the proven ease and rapidity of change by individuals but also the reasoning which goes with it. The majority of individuals will easily re-evaluate their post hoc, convincing themselves that they really chose the line of action and not admitting or even feeling manipulated.

Our cognitive constraints mean that a good deal of what happens is not purposely available, mainly if our attention is directed elsewhere. Two classic studies reveal these occurrences.

In one of such studies, researchers requested participants to watch a video recording of players passing a basketball and count the number of moves by the players wearing white. While the video was running, an individual in a gorilla suit walked across the screen. While concentrating on the instructions and counting the players' moves, most people did not see the gorilla. They could swear that it was not part of the video.

In a similar experiment, a researcher asked random people for instructions. Two other members of the team walked between them, carrying out a doorway throughout the conversation. Also, the initial researcher was swapped for someone else. The research outcome revealed that the individual giving instructions did not observe the switch most of the time.

It is not merely flagrant manipulation, inattention, and post hoc rationalization that could alter our behavior. It turns out we could use an event referred to as 'priming' to change people's behavior with no conscious knowledge of their own.

In reality, researchers have claimed all kinds of priming effects, indicating that we could be manipulated subtly and only with no knowledge on our part. We are apt to assert that any consequent behavior was our choice altogether, mostly because we don't want to feel controlled.

It may not come as a surprise to discover that many of these principles are implemented repeatedly. It is no longer a conspiracy theory. It only represents the individual urge to control and manipulate others to achieve our desires.

Whenever you come across a virtually successful advertisement, one which makes you want to purchase the item, you can be sure you have been manipulated using these fundamentals.

Likewise, according to their faith, when people act in violent ways, they have a reasonably good chance of being manipulated.

Shortly, it might become considerably disturbing. There is already technology that may be employed to deduce your psychological condition through a brain scan and view your thoughts' contents. This is an emerging technology but will improve).

Besides, there are means of implanting behaviors or causing abnormal mental conditions, using transcranial magnetic stimulation (TMS) or ultrasound. These technologies may become more powerful, selective, and prevalent in the not too distant future.

Does this seem like we're always readily manipulated and helpless?

Yes, none of us can forecast how we will behave in challenging situations unless we get an opportunity to examine ourselves. Many people would not wish to experience this type of stress.

Yes, that much of the stuff that manipulates us happens at a level far removed from careful focus. We are excellent at faking our activities. Even those exceptionally out of character' were the consequence of our decisions.

However, no, if you learn how to look closely at your behaviors. Be disciplined, pay conscious attention to your activities to test who is in control. Should you notice yourself behaving or feeling tempted to act in a means that may not be 'you,' try and identify what's happening. Do you truly need to act like this, or does it just feel like you need to?

REVERSE PSYCHOLOGY

WHAT IS REVERSE PSYCHOLOGY

There's a high probability that you have heard the term reverse psychology thrown around. It is a method you probably have used unconsciously, while others have mastered the act. It is a strategy of using someone's thoughts to manipulate them.

Two scientists, Adorno and Horkheimer, initially conceptualized the idea. They both developed the concept of reverse psychology, where individuals respond to the opposite of what they would like to do. They called their concept "Psychoanalysis in Reverse."

Reverse psychology is a standard method applied by individuals to get what they desire or reach their objectives. Even if you have not used it before, you have probably noticed someone else use it. It is not always easy to comprehend reverse psychology once it occurs. For that reason, it is essential to understand just what it is, how it's used, and why and how it functions.

Understanding the meaning of reverse psychology might appear confusing at first glance, but after a careful closer examination, it begins to make sense. The Cambridge English Dictionary defined reverse psychology as "a method of trying to make someone do what you want by asking them to do the opposite and expecting them to disagree with you."

Reverse psychology is a strategy for getting everything you need by demanding or indicating what you do not want. Researchers call it tactical self-anticonformity as your communicated need goes right contrary to what you would like.

The expression also admits that reverse psychology is a strategy. Instead of communicating your wishes right, you conceal them and instead request the opposite of what you would like. If you employ reverse psychology, you use words that indicate what someone should do, though you would like them to do precisely the reverse.

HOW REVERSE PSYCHOLOGY MANIPULATION WORKS

Reverse psychology is an easy idea. You would like somebody to do something but are relatively sure they will not do it even if you ask nicely or directly. So you attempt to manipulate the person into doing it by telling or asking them to do the exact opposite of everything you want them to do.

For instance, if you are trying to get your spouse to paint your bedroom. You could tell him, "Never mind, I'll do the bedroom; after all, I'm a much better painter." The next thing you know, he has a paintbrush in hand, painting, or ready to go.

A lot of people associate reverse psychology with children. Is there any parent who has not used reverse psychology on their child to get them to do something? Like telling a purple-haired teenager the color works on him in hopes, he will instantly dye it to its original color? But people of all ages are vulnerable to the manipulations of reverse psychology.

According to Dr. Jeanette Raymond, a Los Angeles-based licensed psychologist, therapist, and dating specialist reverse psychology frequently works because people need liberty. "It is more empowering to think that you just did something from your very own free will than because you were pressured, threatened, shamed to it, or are terrified of losing that connection."

From the psychotherapeutic angle, reverse psychology is more correctly termed a paradoxical intervention. The expression "reverse psychology" is a media creation, Raymond states. At a paradoxical intervention, a therapist informs a customer to engage in behavior the client is attempting to solve.

If a patient is attempting to become a procrastinator, his counselor might spend 1 hour daily procrastinating. The notion is that this can help the customer focus on the behavior and its potential causes and let him understand that the action is voluntary and, therefore, may be controlled.

There are some worries if paradoxical interventions by a specialist are ethical. Occasionally a patient's difficulty entails pain or anxiety, so requesting the individual to Try and create the fear or pain is not always deemed appropriate.

Reverse psychology, or paradoxical intervention, is a comparatively new concept in psychotherapy. However, it may also be considered a myth. For instance, a parent will always advise the child they don't want to marry the never-do-well she is in love with, for fear she will not marry the loser, but what is their actual intention? However, does this work for everyone and in every circumstance?

Experts tell us that reverse psychology is more inclined to work on people who like to maintain control. People you can describe as rebels, and narcissistic individuals, to list a couple.

Agreeable, more passive individuals generally will do precisely what you ask. Therefore reverse psychology is not required for them. Additionally, it tends to work better on those who Are making decisions based on emotions instead of carefully evaluating situations.

The successful usage of reverse psychology depends more on the character type compared to relationship dynamics. An individual is fighting with individuality and liberty. The paradox might work because that person feels as though they are still resisting by doing precisely what you tell them not to do.

Take Julian Assange as an example. There have been threats on his life from the U.S and other big nations to get him to stop hacking and leaking sensitive government data, but rather than stop, he keeps defying these countries. Would the case have been the same if he was ignored or praised for doing a great job? He probably would not have been too intent.

[12]

The great thing is most of us are not thinking about whether to use reverse psychology to halt the hacking of sensitive government data. No, most of us use it to get relatively benign motives, generally on kids and partners, or in a corporate setting.

If you have kids or work with them, you have likely used a good dose of reverse psychology on them at some point in time. After all, kids are always hard bent on the contrary to what their parents or adults tell them. Like most adults, they do not like being told what to do.

In a particular experiment, 2-year-olds were instructed not to play with a specific toy. Within a short while, the same toy they were supposed to stay away from is what they started playing with. Likewise, in a different experiment, older children were told that they could pick a poster out of a bunch of five. But shortly after that statement, they were informed that among those five, one was not accessible after all.

They unexpectedly found the poster that was missing quite desirable. Some studies also demonstrate that warning labels only make a product more attractive to children, like those on a violent TV show.

Parents may use reverse psychology to dull some of the kids' innate desire to frustrate their fantasies. However, they must do this responsibly and sparingly. To start, if you use reverse psychology too frequently, it is going to become clear and will not work. Your children are going to see you as a manipulator, which is not particularly a great thing.

[13]

Secondly, you should never apply "negative' reverse psychology, which is detrimental to your child's self-esteem. For instance, don't tell your child you will put his bike away for him since he probably can not figure out how to move it in your crowded garage without scratching the car. Instead, start looking for positive kinds of reverse psychology. Let us say your child will not eat dinner. Tell her that is alright, but because dinnertime seemingly is over, it is now bedtime.

With adolescents, often it helps to argue against yourself, in reverse-reverse psychology. If your 16-year-old needs to attend a sketchy-sounding occasion, for example, tell her you can not force her to stay away, even if you have proof there are apparent risks. She will need to decide for herself what is wisest. Now you are effectively arguing on your own, which might cause your kid to take your information ultimately.

The paradox is not permission to precisely what the kid wants instead of what the parent wants. It is about inviting the child to do exactly the wrong thing, so it becomes unpalatable.

Some psychologists tend to be against using reverse psychology under any conditions. If you reward your child for doing precisely the opposite of everything you say, you tell your kid not to cut his hair. He cuts it, and then you tell him how good he looks after the cut. You are teaching the child not to listen to you next time and possibly ever again. You are also teaching him that you do not mean what you say.

HOW TO USE REVERSE PSYCHOLOGY

We have identified reverse psychology as the act of getting another individual to say or do anything by telling them the opposite of what you want to be done. It can be quite effective in advertising and could be useful when dealing with specific sorts of individuals.

However, it would help if you were careful about how and when you apply reverse psychology. It may be regarded as a kind of cynical manipulation. When used routinely, it may damage relationships. Adhere to applying reverse psychology occasionally, and in unserious instances, so it does not lead to some form of abuse.

CHANGE A PERSON'S MIND USING REVERSE PSYCHOLOGY

Start by introducing an alternative. Get this alternative inserted in the other individual's brain. It can be something that the individual would usually not withstand, and they could initially jeer at it. However, you ought to guarantee that the individual is conscious of the choice accessible.

For instance, you are deciding between two events to attend on a Saturday night. Your partner is a movie enthusiast, and their set of friends have a movie night. You are more of a board sports person, and a different group of friends is getting a game night.

Make your buddy aware of the choice you desire. You can say something like, "Did you hear James and Janet do this board game night? Boring, if you ask me."

Use subtle strategies to make the choice appealing.

Figure out ways to make the alternative desirable. Insert subtle suggestions that will create a feeling of desire from another person.

From the previous example, you can casually mention board games that are played in the event. You might play a game of cards with your buddies a couple of days ahead of the event, letting your partner understand how enjoyable the game can be.

You might also make the partner seem more tempting. Bring up exciting memories you had hanging out with James and Janet. Talk about their outstanding qualities. For instance, say something like, James has the best collection of wine in his house, and he tells great stories all the time."

USE NONVERBAL PROMPTS.

For instance, you could play a variant of a board game on your mobile phone for the person. You can encourage James and Janet out for coffee along with the friend before the event, reminding them just how much fun they can be.

DISCOURAGE OR CONTEND AGAINST YOUR DESIRED CHOICE.

When the person looked to have bought the idea, you might become slightly argumentative. This can add the excess push you need to make the individual do everything you desire. They are already somewhat enticed by the alternative. Should you push on that choice now, a resistant individual is very likely to push it longer.

Still, on the previous example, wait till Saturday night comes around. Say something like, "We could visit James and Janet's, or movie night. What do you think? I think James and Janet's thing might be a bit boring."

Now, your partner may push to visit James and Janet's, but if they're still uncertain, try and be more explicit. Say something like, "We can go to James and Janet's next time."

PUSH FURTHER TO GET A DECISION

To conclude the negotiating procedure, you can now push the person to make a choice. The idea here would be to make the person believe that they are making their own choice. Ask them what they would like to do, and wait for a reply. Hopefully, the person will opt for the option you are routing for.

From the example we have been using, say something like, "We could visit James and Janet's, or even the movie night. What do you think? It is your choice."

By allowing your partner to think that it's their choice, they will believe that they are claiming their freedom. You have made James and Janet's party seem tempting. You have also expressed some resistance to it, which a contrary person might push back against it. With luck, your partner will choose James and Janet's event.

EFFECTIVE REVERSE PSYCHOLOGY

UNDERSTAND THE PERSONALITY BEFORE APPLYING REVERSE PSYCHOLOGY

As expected, not everybody responds well to reverse psychology. People who are inclined to be compliant may react better to direct instructions. However, some people are resistant by nature. They are very opinionated and enjoy having their ways. For such people, reverse psychology might work nicely.

Pay attention to the conversation you have had with such a person. Do they tend to go with the flow of things, or do they often resist? Suppose you know a person who's an independent thinker and enjoys withstanding the status quo. In that case, this individual might be more vulnerable to reverse psychology than a generally agreeable person.

You also need to bear this in mind if you're planning on using reverse psychology on kids. In case you have a kid that will be uncooperative, they'll be a lot more inclined to react to reverse psychology than an agreeable child.

USE UNCOMPLICATED REVERSE PSYCHOLOGY

Reverse psychology ought to be lighthearted and funny even. This is particularly true when using the method on young ones. Attempt to use it as a way to make someone believe that they are outwitting you.

Let's say you are trying to get your child to make his bed on time. You could ask him to wait for you to finish brushing your teeth, making him feel you know he needs help making his bed. You are likely to get to the room and find he has already made his bed or is in the process. This is his way of proving to you that he can take care of himself.

The same method can apply when dealing with an adult. Allow the person to think they are claiming their liberty from the circumstance. You could pick between two scenarios, like two types of movies, a foreign film with subtitles versus a comedy.

You really desire to watch a foreign movie. So you can say something like, "I don't think I have the patience and attention span for subtitles." You will be surprised that your friend will choose the foreign movie over the comedy to prove they have a superior attention span.

WHAT DOES THE OTHER PERSON WANT

Before you decide on reverse psychology and the type to use, think of what the other person desires in a particular situation. A more complex variant of reverse psychology could be required sometimes. If somebody's desire to do something outweighs their level of resistance, traditional reverse psychology might backfire.

For instance, your friend wishes to attend a concert in a dangerous part of the city. It may seem like a bad idea, but simple reverse psychology might be inefficient. If you simply say, "You are right. You ought to go. You only live once." He may wholeheartedly concur, as he indeed does desire to be at the concert.

[19]

Try something different, like attempting to argue against yourself in such scenarios, in contrast to the option available. Say something like, "It is really up to you. You have to decide what to do. I am pretty sure this part of the city is dangerous. However, only you can decide what is ideal for you."

You are allowing your friend to consider themselves here. If he is generally resistant, he may rather yield to your advice instead of thinking himself. He might decide against going to that part of town due to the risk involved.

FOCUS ON YOUR OBJECTIVE

Make sure you remain focused at all times by occasionally reminding yourself what you want the person to do. Sometimes, there may be arguments in the process of applying reverse psychology. It's easy to derail off track of your goal during the whole period of a debate. Try to remain on track and remember your preferred result.

WHAT'S REACTANCE?

Reactance is a psychological term that pertains to this uncomfortable feeling that you get when you believe that your freedom has been threatened. When undergoing reactance, the honest answer would be to do the reverse of what is required as a way of expressing your liberty. If you have had your freedom previously and it was suddenly removed, you will probably encounter reactance.

If a parent tells a child they are not permitted to play video games after school while the child has been enjoying this freedom, the child might experience extreme reactance. When that occurs, the child will probably attempt to discover a way to play video games, regardless of their parents' instructions.

Reactance is at the center of reverse psychology. The plan's objective is to make somebody feel this feeling of reactance so they can push back from the specified request. If you have demanded that you do not desire, they will probably do what you need through reactance.

INSTANCES OF REVERSE PSYCHOLOGY

Almost everyone that existed has used reversed psychology one way to the other on someone or has had someone used it on them before. The term "reverse psychology" might now have been mentioned, but the meaning is apparent. Scientists have analyzed reverse psychology, also, and discovered several ways it may be utilized. In marketing and sales, it is used quite blatantly and deliberately.

REVERSE PSYCHOLOGY IN SALES

Several well-known sales techniques are derived from reverse psychology. One is that is the "door in the face" technique. This technique begins when the salesperson delivers an outrageous sales pitch. At some stage, the buyer might feel pressured to buy the product or service been marketed. Nonetheless, this is frequently not the purchase the salesperson is aspiring to create. Instead, they attempt to excite the prospective customer to push and present a lower deal. The customer is very likely to feel much less reactance and much more comfortable in accepting.

For instance, maybe the salesman begins with a pitch about a top-notch vacuum. He goes on and on about all its bells and whistles but mentions that the cost is several thousand bucks. When you express resistance to this, they offer you a more modest vacuum cleaner that now looks like a more sensible purchase for you. This less costly vacuum would be the product they have been attempting to market all along.

REVERSE PSYCHOLOGY IN MARKETING

Reverse psychology in advertising has been growing in popularity among high-end shops. We can see reverse psychology in action by paying attention to how Prade set up one store in Manhattan.

The shop does not have any outside signage. There is nothing that suggests that it is a shop, let alone a reputable Prada shop. This creates the illusion that they are not attempting to sell to just anybody who walks in off the road. You need to know it is there, or you may miss it. This enriches its mysterious sense and feels of exclusivity. Consumers who might feel uneasy with being excluded will be more inclined to pay a visit to the shop and make a buy.

REVERSE PSYCHOLOGY IN KIDS

In our previous examples above, we have discussed in detail how reverse psychology in children works. How it can be harmful and when it can be used effectively.

REVERSE BEHAVIOR IN TEACHING

Teachers frequently use reverse psychology to get their students interested in challenging subjects. This may have very favorable results if used properly. For instance, a teacher who needs their pupils to read a challenging book that is not mandatory might have a better chance by indicating that the book is too tough for pupils or graded in a higher grade level. To establish their instructor's incorrectly, the pupils might attempt to find that book and read it. However, if the instructor merely suggested they ought to read it, few would likely do this.

REVERSE BEHAVIOR IN RELATIONSHIPS

Reverse psychology in relationships may end up being an issue. It may come across as a manipulative means to get exactly what you would like at the expense of your spouse. Here is an example; assume you wanted your partner to visit the shop for you. Afterward, instead of merely requesting them straight, you let them know that they likely can not deal with the traffic. If they think you think that way, they may do it just to prove you wrong.

There are many issues with this situation. First, suppose you use this technique regularly. In that case, your spouse may start losing faith in your words and eventually become mad if they think you are attempting to control them. Alternately, using reverse psychology in relationships could backfire. Rather than fighting back, they might think about what you said and believe it. They may quit driving in traffic and finally become dependent on you for all their transport, losing faith in their abilities after a time.

DOES REVERSE BEHAVIOR WORK?

Reverse psychology may get the job done. In reality, in two studies, researchers reasoned that reverse psychology could reach its target sometimes. In other circumstances, however, reverse psychology does not work. Several factors need to be in play for reverse psychology to be effective; the target person must believe the deception. They need to believe that you need them to do something before they respond by doing the contrary. Additionally, they should not realize you are using reverse psychology. Ultimately, some men and women are more vulnerable to reverse psychology compared to others.

DRAWBACKS OF REVERSE PSYCHOLOGY?

Reverse psychology may have some horrible side-effects. Should you use it too frequently, it may lead other people to distrust you. Should you use it in a close relationship, then you might miss the chance to be genuine about yourself. Should you use it for important conclusions, you might rob the other individual of this opportunity to have a voice in something which matters. Furthermore, if used too much, it might rob you, with time, of your capability to communicate efficiently and directly since you rely increasingly more on ambiguous communicating methods such as reverse psychology.

HYPNOTISM

When you think about hypnosis, you probably imagine an old black and white movie with the antagonist swinging a pocket watch back and forth. Do you think hypnosis can get the job done? Researchers state that believing is half the procedure.

There is a great deal of skepticism and distrust around the topic of hypnotism, particularly in Western cultures. This skepticism stems partially from hypnosis used as amusement and from many initial notions on the subject.

THE HISTORY OF HYPNOTISM

Hypnotism is an extremely contentious subject because it is shrouded in numerous myths and misconceptions. Despite the conclusive scientific study of its widespread clinical usage, many people are terrified by hypnotism and hooked on the stigma around it. Let's first go through a brief history of hypnotism's roots and development to break down a number of those thoughts.

The study and use of hypnotism have been in practice in the US as far back as the mid-1800. It dates back to early historic times. Hypnosis is indivisible from western psychology and medicine. Its usage is available in Roman, Persian, Greek, Indian, Egyptian, Chinese, and Sumerian cultures. One of the early publications that talked about hypnotism is the famous Sanskrit book The Law of Mandu. It spoke of " Sleep-Walking," "Dream-sleep," and Ecstacy-Sleep.

Throughout the Middle Ages, kings and princes were widely thought to possess the power of healing, also called the "royal." It's recorded that they conducted supernatural healings known as "magnetism" or "mesmerism." Dr. Paracelsus was the first individual to use magnets to perform healing in the 16th century. This technique of supernatural healing became famous, taking to the 18th century.

It was then the Physician Franz Mesmer found he could instigate a trance without magnetic drive. Mesmer erroneously reasoned that the healing powers came out of an invisible force besides the magnets. Maybe you've heard somebody say something mesmerizing?

Mesmer was the first to spell out a ritualistic way of hypnotism, which he handed to his devotees, that continued to develop the method. Regrettably, Frank Mesmer is why we have such a mysterious view of hypnosis today. He had a few relatively strange and evasive practices to his approaches, like wearing a cloak and playing odd music throughout the ritual.

Other doctors believed that hypnosis was not a magical power but an implemented trance that opened the mind. The growth and development of hypnosis carried on without Mesmer's odd ways. Throughout history, many have thought hypnosis to be a powerful emotional solution to many ailments of the body and mind. Seeing the potential of hypnosis in the healthcare field, many notable physicians risked their medical licenses to pioneer its use within their practices.

A priest, Abbe Faria, started to study the authenticity of hypnotism around 1813. The Priest suggested that it was not magnetism or any external forces that led to a trance but instead the mind. Faria's strategy formed the basis for the French hypnosis-psychotherapy institution's theoretical and clinical work, the Nancy School, also referred to as the School of Suggestion.

Ambroise-Auguste Liebault, the Nancy School founder, thought hypnosis was a psychological occurrence and ignored magnetism theories. He concentrated his research and hypnosis training on the difference between being asleep and in a trance. He reasoned that hypnosis is a state of mind made by suggestion. From this concept, he wrote Sleep and its Analogous States in 1866. His work drew a number of the notable trailblazers of psychology to study in the Nancy School.

During the summit of hypnotism, many doctors used hypnosis for anesthesia. In 1821, Recamier became renowned for inducing hypnotic trance on a patient for anesthesia in major surgery. After more than a decade, the British surgeon John Elliotson, who proposed using the stethoscope in England, reported several painless surgeries using hypnosis.

Taking more than a century to accomplish this, physicians and researchers eventually could eliminate the blot Mesmer left behind in the practice of hypnosis, showing it as a legitimate clinical technique. From the end of the 19th century, both physicians and medical universities researched and implemented hypnosis with patients and studies for a plethora of health anomalies.

Despite having lots of predecessors in this area of study, the Scottish ophthalmologist James Braid is ascribed as the "father of modern hypnotism." He coined the expression neuro-hypnotism, meaning nervous sleep. This expression was later shortened to hypnotism in 1841. Within another century, hypnosis was integrated into the medical practice for quick treatment after WWI and WWII.

Centuries later, documentation and development through contemporary technology have helped discover the reality. By using brain imaging, doctors and researchers can actually observe that hypnotherapy is a state. It's not a trance, nor can it be vacant. On the contrary, it's a real frame of mind where the topic is quite receptive to change and accepting new thoughts, which a very conscious state was trained to block.

HYPNOSIS AND SCIENCE

From the historical study of hypnosis, we have discovered it is a product of scientific investigation. It has been established that hypnosis works. However, what are the consequences of a hypnotic session in today's world? The Director of the Program at Placebo Studies at Harvard Medical School, Irving Kirsch, believes there are still many hypnosis myths, mostly from the way the subject is presented in the media.

Aside from such preconceived prepositions, hypnosis is a well-studied and recognized treatment method. Hypnotism is used for treatments ranging from stress management to choosing healthy lifestyle habits.

Talking more about weight loss, Kirsch's group found that those patients that bunch cognitive behavior therapy (CBT) with hypnosis lose more weight than people who did not. After four to six months, those who employed CBT with hypnosis dropped more than twenty-five pounds while those just using CBT dropped ten pounds.

In any case, the hypnosis-tested team sustained that weight reduction for eighteen months later, whereas the other group could not.

Besides supporting weight loss, there are bits of proof that hypnosis is successful in the transitory alleviation of the pain. Len Milling, a professor at the University of Hartford and clinical psychologist, additionally reasoned that entrancing might help decrease post-surgical pain in children and distress related to other clinical cycles.

Stanford University School of Medicine's Doctor David Spiegel, a research professional, and psychiatry and behavioral sciences professor, had some fascinating information added. He explained: "Half the people I see once ceased smoking, half of them will not touch a cigarette for two years.

His conclusion is supported by the Nicotine and Tobacco Research in a 2007 research work, where over 20% of 286 patients stopped smoking following hypnotic therapy. By comparison, just 14% stopped while employing regular behavioral counseling. The hypnotic treatment was immensely successful in patients having a history of depression and stress.

Having said that, trying to highlight precisely how hypnosis is powerful is catchy. If you ask ten different accredited therapists how it's been successfully applied, you will likely get ten different answers. Although several experts agree on one common thing, that to hypnotize somebody, it happens in 2 primary phases. The first phase is often known as induction. The next stage is the suggestion.

Throughout the induction, patients are usually told to attempt to unwind. The doctor will inform them to concentrate on the fact that they are entering a hypnotized state. The suggestion phase entails subtly proposing thoughts to the individual to solve unhealthy behaviors or feelings. Patients are given situations to help them envision hypothetical situations as though they were actual. The kinds of hints and prompts provided change by the sort of patient and their particular treatment needs.

In many ways, hypnosis may be contrasted to mindfulness techniques and practices because it compels the individual to enter a deeper rumination state. Spiegel stated that "While many people fear losing control in hypnosis, it's, in actuality, a way of enhancing mind-body control."

These days you could get everything out of a seminar, like how to stop smoking and overeating. The real question is, how practical are these instructions? Suppose the clinical study and recorded advancement of hypnosis have something to say regarding the topic. In that case, an individual can be set in a hypnotic state to change their thoughts about a custom.

This is the area where specialists say you need to think of the capability to become hypnotized as the starting point. Otherwise, your conscious condition will hamper any attempt to move your mind to a hypnotic state.

A hypnotic state makes it possible to enter a degree of awareness your conscious state can't reach, thereby showing your emotional barriers and enabling you to be more receptive to the ways around them.

STATE OF HYPNOSIS AND HYPNOTHERAPY

Hypnosis is a state of consciousness like what you experience when sleeping, intoxicated, or dreaming. The experience is not the same for everyone. Instead, it is unique to each person at different times. So although you will find attributes of this state common among hypnotized individuals, it's never the same from one individual to another, nor can it be the same whenever the same person is hypnotized.

Like the other states, a hypnotic trance is tremendously influenced by setting and set. The set and setting refer to this mindset and environment that an individual has during the encounter.

Many people who would have tried hypnotherapy are put off by what the media show them, mostly "staged hypnotism," for the camera. They fear losing control and do something clumsy or, better still, come out with an unpleasant feeling. It's a preconceived stigma thing. However, most of the time, you are in control, and the whole experience is the reverse of what you feared.

People today tend to undergo some common beliefs and thought processes while getting hypnosis for healing purposes. This description is not likely to be a specific match for every single hypnotic subject all the time, nevertheless. If you're thinking about hypnotherapy, it will provide you a good idea about what to expect.

IT STARTS WITH RELAXATION

Relaxation is the state of freeing your mind and body from tension and anxiety, which is a crucial hypnosis characteristic. Hypnosis does not mainly make your body and mind relaxed. Instead, the process of hypnosis induction requires freeing your body and mind of every heaviness in response to the suggestion of the hypnotherapist.

For instance, the hypnotherapist might indicate a sense of heaviness in a couple of portions of the body. Hypnosis is a teamwork between the hypnotherapist and the client. You may feel inclined to observe a sense of heaviness in the body area suggested. But, it's your responsibility to cause relaxation rather than the therapist.

Contrary to how hypnosis has been portrayed, where a hypnotic subject carries out a hypnotist's orders, the hypnotherapist's suggestions are generally an invitation, not a command. As you consider the suggestions the hypnotherapist makes, you may end up thinking something like, "Truly, it could be quite wonderful to relax at the moment," then find it relatively easy to let go of anxiety and unwind. There's no "must" or "have to" in the process.

FOCUS ON THE ISSUE

Focus is another quality required in the hypnosis process. This is also the hypnotized person's responsibility and not the therapist who only tries to suggest.

Hypnotherapy typically occurs in a private, quiet area. Focusing on the therapist's voice is generally relatively straightforward and natural. Many people find it easy to let go of distractions and concentrate on their focus on the hypnotherapist's topic, which is why they are there in the first place.

The therapist is trained to direct your thought processes in a particular manner that's proven beneficial in overcoming addictive behavior, controlling pain, or assisting with many different psychological, emotional, and behavioral issues. Individuals under hypnosis will concentrate on just what the therapist is saying.

The therapist will go over what's going to happen with the subject before he starts communicating. You would have already discussed why you are trying to find therapy and your hypnotherapist's treatment objectives.

The therapist may direct the process to let you think about your addiction and associated issues in a concentrated way. However, since care is required to make sure that you are calm and relaxed, it is not mostly overwhelming—the information you have to focus on is usually direct and unambiguous.

OPEN YOUR MIND

A vital facet of hypnosis would be to try to generate a state of increased susceptibility. When people take part in counseling for addictive behaviors, they usually think of numerous reasons why the counselor's most useful suggestions won't function. It can grow to be a very long string of "yes, buts..."

When individuals are under hypnosis, they frequently become more receptive to thinking about possibilities than within their normal, wide-awake state. In some individuals, this open-mindedness may result in a heightened awareness of personal power. The individual realizes that they are capable of more than they previously believed possible.

Again, this open-mindedness should not be confused with a lack of control. Although individuals under hypnosis may find themselves thinking about matters they would not generally, they do not typically do whatever will violate their value system. Instead, there's a feeling of possibilities that were not evident earlier, coupled with a willingness to see things otherwise.

SENSORY CHANGE

Hypnosis is well-known for its capacity to induce strange sensory experiences, most importantly, allowing people to experience sensations like pain differently from normal. This result is so deep that some individuals have undergone surgery with no anesthetic. It may also create differences in how you experience visuals and auditory sensations.

Much like other hypnosis facets, these changes have been controlled by the individual under hypnosis, maybe not by the hypnotherapist, who's merely offering hints. For instance, pain perception has been strongly affected by the individual's stress level in pain. Many people discover that without the stress present at a state of profound relaxation, they can't disconnect from pain, which results in detachment.

SEPARATION

With hypnosis, a few people experience detachment or dissociation, like they are somewhat removed from what they are experiencing. Today, many people describe this as watching themselves outside or as a character on a TV screen. Even at that, individuals under hypnosis continue to know about where they are and what they are doing at all times.

This sense of detachment can vary from feeling involved in the hypnotic procedure yet viewing it from an external perspective concurrently, turning back and forth between viewing from the outside to becoming involved in the adventure. Some people do not get this observer effect in any way, whereas, for others, it's incredibly apparent. For some, it feels like an out of body experience.

STAGES OF HYPNOSIS

Hypnosis is a safe procedure broadly recognized by medical and scientific specialists to affect lives positively. If you would like to be happier, more confident, healthier, and have less stress in your lifetime, then Hypnosis is a solution you may need to look into.

The hypnotic effect occurs when an individual is so intensely concentrated; it enables the subconscious mind's boundless capability to act beyond the perceived constraints, causing physical and psychological alterations.

There are different stages in the hypnosis process, and we will be looking at taking an in-depth look at each.

INDUCTIONS

How can a hypnotherapist get their client into a state of relaxation? How can a stage hypnotist hypnotize volunteers throughout a staged show? In either case, it comes down to a technique called the hypnotic induction'.

This is the stage an individual is guided into a hypnotic state. The hypnotist/hypnotherapist can then use various state deepeners to ensure the subject is satisfactorily hypnotized and follow the suggestions given to them throughout the session.

PROGRESSIVE HYPNOTIC INDUCTIONS

There are several distinct varieties of induction. Some occur within minutes, while others take merely a few seconds. The most typical induction for either hypnotherapy and stage hypnosis is a "progressive induction," also known as "progressive relaxation induction." As you may anticipate, the induction process is somewhat slow and gradual, involving various parts.

The hypnotherapist will speak with their client, providing them distinct suggestions and requesting them to follow their instructions. Progressive hypnotic inductions can involve suggestions about many things, such as;

Breathing

"Concentrate on your breathing, and let every single breath you let out relax you more..."

Muscular relaxation

'Allow each of the muscles in your upper body to relax gradually. Your chest, your belly, your shoulders, and your arms. Free all of them completely now...'

Tension and Relaxation

"Now, squeeze all of the muscles in your legs tight, in the hips to your feet... Hold it down for a few seconds, now release the muscles. Notice just how much more relaxed your whole lower body is now..."

Visualization

"Imagine you are in an awesome, relaxing location... your ideal place of complete comfort... Notice how relaxed you feel as you can enjoy simply unwinding now in that special..." location in your mind.

Counting

"With every number I count, allow yourself to go deeper into the state of trance... starting with 10..."

These methods rely only on the usage and approval of hypnotic suggestions. Some customers may react better to the physical suggestions, calming the muscles. Others might participate more with visual suggestions, and some might prefer the more analytic and cognitive procedures.

There are many versions of the facets, as mentioned above, of a progressive hypnotic induction. These are the most commonly applied, and they are acceptable by most clients because they take away all the myths around hypnotism.

You may feel that a progressive hypnotic induction seems easy enough to perform, and you might be quite right to think that. It mainly boils down to asking a client to do something and indicating it in a simple way to comprehend and follow. Nevertheless, some hypnotic inductions demand somewhat more than merely speaking to the client whenever they got their eyes shut.

EYE FIXATION INDUCTION

Another type of hypnotic induction is the "eye fixation." This is where the therapist tells the client to look deep into something, like an image or light. The idea behind this process is that, as the client focuses on the image and follows the therapist's instruction, their eyes become tired. This is the point where the hypnotist introduces manipulations or suggestions through their voice.

The hypnotherapist then implies that the customer shuts their eyes and gradually fall into a trance-like state.

FAST INDUCTIONS

Another popular kind of induction is "rapid induction." As the name suggests, this usually means a "fast induction" process. Quick inductions are more often employed by stage and road-side hypnotists since they tend to be dramatic-looking. However, in recent times, this method is also getting increasingly more widely used by hypnotherapists.

Quick induction is a terrific method of cutting the induction process short, providing a therapist longer time to get into the therapy component.' Additionally, rapid hypnotic inductions help work with hypnotherapy clients. A more extended, more relaxation-based' strategy might not be suitable if you have a couple of minutes to operate or if the customer is in severe pain. There are 3 Distinct categories of rapid hypnotic induction:

Shock inductions

Shock induction occurs when a therapist as the client engage in something then give them a sudden instruction, like a jolt telling them to "sleep." This causes the customer to enter a state of trance instantly. Instead of attempting to know why the jolt happened and cope with their "fight-flight," it is more comfortable to "sleep."

Although, we know hypnosis is not the same as sleeping. However, shock induction uses the word, and it has become connected with hypnosis in many movies and books.

Confusion inductions

The application of confusion through rapid hypnotic inductions is quite much like the usage of shock. The point is to set the client in a state where they are overloaded' and unable to continue to concentrate. You can request them to count backward from 10,000 in leaps of 37 while transferring one hand in one direction, another in another direction, and singing their replies to their favorite song' (Sounds confusing?)

If you engage the client in numerous activities, they will end up bloated and confused. Also, the choice to only sleep' is a lot more preferable than attempting to keep on engaging with the perplexing procedure.

Pattern disturbance inductions

These hypnotic inductions involve suggesting handshakes or any form of physical contact interruption. The notion is that you disrupt a "subconscious routine." If that routine is disrupted, there's a moment in which the customer's mind is confused and does not know what is happening. It is at the point where you let them "sleep" or fall into a trance.

CONVERSATIONAL HYPNOTIC INDUCTIONS

Some hypnotherapists opt not to utilize a formal induction procedure whatsoever and instead take part in something called "conversational hypnosis." It's possible to use conversational hypnosis methods to get the same effect as a typical hypnotic induction. But it's more covert and indirect.

Conversational hypnotic inductions involve speaking to the client about any topic even if it is not related to their therapy and interspersing and imitating various hypnotic suggestions in whatever it's stated. Here's an example of a conversational hypnotic induction.

'Thank you for coming in today. It is good to see you are beginning to unwind even though we have only just sat down. Most say they enter hypnosis almost immediately; they sit. Maybe it's the seat or something... it's a comfortable feeling to understand that you can just unwind as you sit on my couch. So, I wonder if now you will fall into a trance earlier or later. But, we do not have to think about moving into hypnosis just yet since we can have a conversation for a few minutes longer until you enter hypnosis. We would not want one to relax into hypnosis too soon, not until precisely when you're all set.'

Many hypnotherapists use these conversational/Ericksonian/indirect approaches during the start of a hypnotherapy session. The pre-hypnosis component prime the customer for more induction. Other folks use these approaches throughout the whole session with no formal hypnotic induction. Many customers will anticipate and prefer to know when a procedure commences.

DEEPENER

Deepening is the method most commonly used right after the hypnotic induction. This can be an essential method to help attain a state of open, deep trance, which allows for more successful suggestions.

As we delve deeper into the topic, we will have to clear up a couple of misconceptions about hypnosis, especially deepening. Several people have shown concern about the concept being a state of "deep" hypnosis, which usually means they are in a helpless state in which the hypnotist has complete control over them and may suggest "anything," even a thing against their character.

This misconception often stems from movies, staged hypnotism, and pop culture references of hypnosis, misinformed or intentionally using tropes for a striking effect. Being "deep" in hypnosis does not imply you will lose control of your memory or that the hypnotist will have absolute control of you or your body.

Hypnotherapists frequently use the expression "deep" but around the depth of hypnosis. The subject is in a state where they are responsive and open to suggestions from the specialist. The more profound the customers go into entrancing, the more responsive they are to change. Therapists employ deepening techniques to help get the client inside that open and responsive state rapidly.

Hypnotic deepening is usually done right after the induction. It can also be performed throughout the session and might be only a brief suggestion or even a longer one, a more formal procedure. It is not a necessary part of hypnotherapy, but most hypnosis will utilize deepeners to ensure the customer is receptive to more work under hypnosis. Here's what a simple process of deepening looks like.

After a client has entered into a trance and gone through the induction procedure, the hypnotherapist might further decide they would like to deepen the hypnotic trance. Among the most frequently used forms of deepener is the classic "staircase" deepener. In this, the hypnotherapist guides the client through a mental picture of them descending a staircase. They usually start by describing the stairs in detail, so the customer has a powerful mental image in their mind.

A few other therapists want to count down from 20, but the specific number is not important. At every step, the customer is motivated to double their psychological relaxation. When they get to the stairs' base, they have attained an extremely calm and relaxed state.

The hypnotherapist counts down the stairs, providing carefully worded suggestions to relax further and let go of concerns. When they get to the base of the stairs, the deepener is perfected. The therapist may decide on the next phase from that point.

The deepener we only went over is among the most common styles, but there are many different approaches for deepening a hypnotic trance. Hypnotherapists tend towards utilizing relaxing, straightforward techniques because they are best for therapeutic applications. The stairs deepener is one such strategy.

There are many others, like the fractionalization method, where the client is taken in and out of a trance, progressive relaxation, which you might have already practiced as a member of a yoga club or yoga progress), along with a very simple countdown, or alternative types of visualization based deepeners.

On the flip side, a stage hypnotist may be more enthusiastic about delighting or surprising his volunteers and viewers. Rather than relaxing, they may attempt to use a surprise or shock based induction and steer clear of the relaxing deepeners all together, as they don't make for a fantastic show.

MOST COMMON TYPES OF DEEPENING

There are several different formats for hypnotic deepening. We are going to look at the most popular one here.

Numerical Deepeners

All these are deepeners that rely on numbers. You count down or up. It involves merely counting down from up or 3 to 10. The counting provides a predetermined amount of time where the deepening can happen, allowing the mind to change. Typical suggestions like "deeper and deeper," "deep sleep," and "relax;" will be made alongside the numbers to help ensure the deepening.

Natural Phenomena Deepeners

The most frequent natural phenomena hypnotic deepener employs the ideomotor response to reunite a limb to normalcy after induction via an Arm levitation or Limb catalepsy induction. A lesser instance of a pure phenomenon deepener provides deepening suggestions as the client exhales to gain from the simultaneous physical suggestions made by breathing out.

Visual Participation Deepeners

This type of deepening occurs by supporting the individual to focus internally on a particular image, typically a trip or preferred location. This creates dissociation from the present environment and might help accessibility source conditions, such as relaxation, further deepening the individual under therapy.

Dissociative Deepeners

All these are deepeners that specifically promote separation, the dissociation of the individual from their present time/space. Many people assert that dissociation is the cornerstone of hypnosis, so anything that supports it is probably useful. A typical illustration of dissociation deepening is requesting the individual to envision drifting from the physical. This can easily result in a visual involvement deepener, like a trip to a favorite location.

Triggered & Conditioned Deepeners

These are somewhat different from the other sorts of deepener. It was not meant to procedure deepening when it was initially introduced. Instead, it set a signal for deepening at a subsequent stage. The triggered word could be "sleep," "relax," "Now," or something suggestive in that line.

The cue term is used to take back the individual to the state where the cue phrase was set up. To this end, the hypnotherapist will appear to set up as deep a trance as can be before installing the word. Such deepening phrases are tools to be implemented by the hypnotherapist when trance depth was interrupted by something, or an excess piece of deepening is needed.

SUGGESTIONS

A suggestion is when an individual is guided by the therapist to react to Ideas for changes in subjective experiences, alterations in perception, feeling, emotion, thought, or behavior during a state of hypnosis.

The suggestion is what contributes to the fascinating effects of hypnosis. For instance, if somebody with a debilitating arm is hypnotized, they might feel relaxed and focused. It's not till they are provided a suggestion like "your arm is starting to feel numb and insensitive" that they start to experience pain relief. The same is true for different kinds of suggestions also.

Suggestions can be direct, or they may be indirect. For example, "you may start to notice changes in the way your arm is feeling." One concept is that suggestions work by changing our expectancies and expectations of what's going to occur. We then have experiences per our longings.

TYPES OF HYPNOTIC SUGGESTIONS

Direct

Direct hypnotic suggestions are those which are apparent and directly said to the client. They are not mystical or ambiguous. Neither are they intended to make the client think. They are easy and straightforward. A good instance of a direct suggestion is "walk for 15 minutes daily, and you will feel energized and pleased with yourself."

Indirect

Indirect hypnosis ideas are more inference, ambiguous, and could have several meanings. A good example is: "you have been encountering challenges in your life since you came into this world. You are quite good at it. I understand there's a remedy for this issue, possibly in the deeper portions of your thoughts, and I question whether it is going to show up earlier in the session or much later into the session."

FEATURES OF EFFECTIVE HYPNOTIC SUGGESTIONS

Straightforward

Hypnotic suggestions should be short and straight to the point, with a single directive or thought. The brain enjoys clarity. So, make it brief and go direct to the point. It makes it effortless for the mind to comprehend.

Practical

The hypnotic suggestion should request the client to do more or less of something. It makes the suggestion practical. The mind enjoys the capability to envision. Hence the suggestion should be simple to envision.

Present Tense

Avoid using the future tense. For instance, use "I do 20-minute push up" instead of "I will do a 20-minute push up". The word "Will" is a future tense, and the subconscious mind is literal in its translation. So, a hypnotic suggestion that includes future tense won't be as effective compared with the one that uses the present tense.

Believable

The suggestion ought to be reasonable. For example, a hypnosis suggestion that says you will grow an arm overnight is not valid. One that pushes clients from the comfort zone, however, is useful. Making suggestions believable is part of the hypnotist's responsibility. It also creates confidence in the client.

Be Positive

Suggestions should focus on the positive. That which is desired rather than what's not. For instance, "I really don't wish to be this worried" may be written as "I feel peaceful and calmer." The mind is favorably oriented. Anything we focus on grows, so the suggestion has to be positively expressed. It is how the brain functions.

Reward

A reward ought to be tied into the suggestion. For instance, "I practice my yoga session 30 minutes per day and feel peaceful and serene." Rewards plus a positive feedback loop are an intrinsic part of how the brain works. The best reward is inherent - something that's an intrinsic part of the task itself. An inherent reward for walking is feeling better. A non-intrinsic reward will be losing weight, which does not occur to some measurable or significant degree for a couple of weeks.

Measurable

Measurable suggestions help the individual know when they are successful. A good illustration of quantifiable suggestion includes "each morning I do 20 push-ups and feel energized." The mind loves to be aware it is successful. A good therapist will create rewards that provide the clients with the satisfaction of a job well done to affect the positive feedback mechanism.

SUGGESTION IN OUR DAILY LIFE

The phenomenon of suggestibility is not only applicable within hypnotic contexts. There are ample instances to indicate that humans are, to a large extent, shaped to have a responsive behavior to things implied. An "Enter" sign in a bank is an example. It is a suggestion, direct and straightforward. However, a suggestion such as "High Voltage" is not as direct. As informative as it may sound, it is not intended to be purely so because the "High Voltage" sign does not assume that you do not know a thing about electricity. What it actually says is "be careful, it is dangerous in here" or "stay away from this area" or "you may get hurt."

In some instances, the suggestions are even more subtly put. Have you been to an automated cash machine gallery? The first thing likely to greet you is the potpourri of humans lined up, edging slowly to the cash machine for withdrawals. You do not merely ignore the queue of humans and walk up to the machine to make your withdrawal, of course. What you do is join the queue; either that, or you leave. In essence, without it being explicitly stated anywhere, you get the suggestion on arrival: wait your turn, fellow, or leave if you cannot wait.

In most of the things we do, convention plays an important role (as a practice widely observed within a society) and experience. Our previous experiences consist of what we have been predisposed to and inform how we perceive things. When you hand a cab driver a $5 note for a fee of $4.15, and he rolls his eyes and asks, "have you got the 15 cents?" you do not get startled, even though you just handed him an amount more than sufficient to foot your bill. This is because you understand that his question is only suggestive of one thing: he wants to hand you your balance, but he is running low on change. The suggestion can be extended further to mean, "you leave the change for him as a tip." or "Pay the exact amount for your ride."

"This way, please" is another example. It is a phrase you may hear if you frequent five-star hotels. An individual you most likely have never seen before beckons on you that way, and you follow without asking questions. On the one hand, it is the absolute reality that you are following someone you do not know that you are entrusting your safety to a stranger. You must have watched enough Crime TV to realize it is not advisable to follow a stranger. As a matter of fact, you would not do this in a different setting. On the other hand, the suggestion is induced by previous experience, that said stranger is connected to the establishment. Hence, you hear "Pease follow me while I show you to your room" and nothing sinister.

Contexts are essential to suggestibility. Interpretation of suggestion is influenced by several factors such as tone, the environment, weather, style of dressing, time of the day, age, perceived status, and self-presentation.

Worthy of note at this point is the fact that sometimes, suggestions thrive on the platform of extremity. There are instances where suggestions are so extreme that they may surpass the believability threshold but delivered with an assertive tone and padded up with feasible conditions. The odds are that they would be accepted as true by certain persons who would assume that such "assertion" would not be made if it were not true.

It is not just about the extremity of the suggestion made, but also about the person's state to whom it is made. Suggestions can thrive on desperation: a young graduate desperate for a job is likely to give in to the suggestion that if he provides a certain sum of money, he could be provided with a dream job. This is how most fraudsters work. They exploit both factors: extremity and desperation.

EFFECTIVE SUGGESTIONS

Perhaps the most crucial point to note when it comes to suggestions is that it must be what the individual receiving the suggestion wanted, and not just a mare suggestion or a statement of fact. The suggestion should be believable either in real life or during a hypnotherapy session. The individual should want what is suggested to be as it is said and be willing to make it.

Sometimes it seems easy for a salesperson to sell you a particular product, like a car. When you are indecisive, he could tell you are undecided but know you want the car. After all, that is why you at the car shop. While you are there moving back and forth in the store, still checking, he then throws in a suggestion in the form of information.

The salesperson informs you that the car's price will be marked up in a few days, but you can get it at the current price if you decide right away. He goes further to tell you more about the car's features and how it's a "limited edition." Perhaps it is a special edition that will not be replicated or has a durable engine than usual, or even a more extended guarantee. The salesperson can pretty much make any suggestion he likes to make you want the car.

He would pick the salesman's evaluation of what you may react to, but it's all suggestion. Obviously, the trick is that you need to get this car, and you have to purchase it with no delay before someone else does. You need that suggestion to warrant spending your money. Therefore, His words hit a home run because you would like to purchase the vehicle.

SOME WORDS TO MAKE SUGGESTION EFFECTIVE

These words are persuasive during hypnotherapy sessions and in life generally.

Because

The word because it is quite strong. It is surreptitious in its simple nature and regular usage. "Because" offers a motive into this subconscious mind for the word to be authentic. It makes the sentence fair, plausible, and appealing to the subconscious thoughts.

Wonder & Curious

Saying " I wonder" or "I'm curious" to someone instantly originates a subconscious response or reaction from them.

Imagine

The word "imagine" creates a mental picture. If a salesperson, an inscription, an advert, or a therapist uses the word, they are trying to create a mental image that your brain immediately responds to by attempting to do just the same.

You/Your Name

You, as well as the more personal version, your real name is quite hypnotic. It has been said that there is nothing sweeter compared to the sound of your name. As soon as we hear our name, we are fascinated.

The More

The more you read this book, the more you're interested in knowing about hypnosis and the power of the mind. The more is a potent hypnotic word that allows the hypnotist to construct a phrase in on another one. That is very similar to As.

As

"As you listen to the sound of my voice." This is a standard line used in hypnotherapy. It's simple to focus your attention inward and unwind even more. This is similar to "The More."

Pretend or Simply Pretend

Pretend is a hypnotic word. It's initiating subconscious thoughts. Pretend that you are going deeply relaxed and detect how great that feels. Pretend works as it takes the strain from the client to do things perfectly. Just pretend you are doing it correctly, and they will probably begin doing it correctly.

SIGNIFICANCE OF WELL DESIGNED SUGGESTIONS

It's essential to understand the significance of a well craft-crafted suggestion in hypnosis and how to produce them. Here are top class rules to follow in creating quality suggestions that work.

Avoid Complexity

For your suggestion to convey the right message, you must communicate clearly because the subconscious works literarily. Avoid making statements like, "When you lay your head on the pillow, it will feel fluffy and soft." While this may seem like a clear and direct statement, the subconscious will wonder if it's the head on the pillow that will feel soft and fluffy.

Positive Phrasing

It is pertinent to stay clear from negative words, especially powerful ones that convey impossibility such as won't, can't, shouldn't, wouldn't, didn't. In some instances, t may be unavoidable to use negative words in some cases, but it has to be used abstractly. you can phrase something like, "you will no longer find the need to cheat." The abstract here is "no longer."

Intensify Interest

Any suggestion we make for hypnotherapy should stimulate intense interest. If the intensity of interest lacks in the listener, it will most likely be ineffective. It has to state what the person wants to take place.

Produce the Existence of Emotion

The existence of emotion is essential to the approval of hypnotic suggestion. The presence of emotion helps hypnotic suggestions to succeed. Although the emotion could be negative or positive, we might also make the emotion of joy by producing impressive suggestions that an individual enjoys hearing.

Don't Create Conscious Objections.

When we phrase a suggestion against an individual's wishes, such a suggestion is very likely to be rejected. If we don't bypass the conscious vital faculty, then it's even more probable. We always ensure that our suggestions are to the point and don't assume whatever might not be agreeable to this listener.

TERMINATION

When an individual is in a trance or a hypnotic state, and the therapist has achieved his goal for that session successfully, the next phase is to bring the individual out of the hypnotic state. The most common method used is through a count down. However, you can count down with a mix of suggestions.

Here's a sample script you can use to terminate a hypnotic state.

Now, I will count from one to five, after which I will say, Totally awake." Your eyes are open by the count of five, and you're then completely conscious, feeling calm, relaxed, refreshed, rested.

- All right. One: slowly, calmly, readily, you are returning to your whole consciousness once more.

- Two: every nerve and muscle in your body is loose and limps relaxed, and you genuinely feel wonderfully great.

- Three: From head to toe, you're feeling great whatsoever. Physically perfect, emotionally ideal, emotionally calm, and tranquil.

- On number four, your eyes start to feel sparkling. On my next count, eyelids open, completely conscious, feeling calm, relaxed, refreshed, relaxed, invigorated, filled with energy.

- Five: You are fully aware of your environment. Eyelids open. Just take a nice, deep breath, then fill your lungs up, and then stretch.

SECRET HYPNOSIS FOR MIND CONTROL - COVERT HYPNOSIS

A covert hypnosis technique is the one in which an individual is hypnotized without their knowledge. It generally takes place during a dialogue.

The thought that somebody can control our thoughts using their words freaks out a lot of people. They forget that we have been secretly hypnotized in one way or another.

While growing, our lives were an interval of hypnosis through which we obtained the beliefs of those around us. So long as you maintain exercising your conscious thinking power, you are going to be alright.

COVERT HYPNOTIC METHODS

You might be thinking about how a person can hypnotize you using only words and probably quickly conclude that it was not possible. The underlying principle of all of the covert hypnotic methods is just like that in conventional hypnosis. It entails evading mindful filtering and allowing the information to get to the subconscious.

Following are the most frequently used covert hypnotic techniques.

KEYWORDS

Some keywords and phrases directly serve as subconscious orders. They force us to put aside our critical thinking faculties. Examples include words such as "relax" or "imagine."

These words are orders our subconscious instantly acts on until we could consciously decide not to. That is if our mind is not obsessed with something else.

Visual images are the most potent type of suggestions, and that is the main reason visualization is indeed powerful. When I ask you to envision something, I am programming your mind with anything I would like you to picture.

If you are still trying to determine how a simple word such as this may program your brain, think about this hypothetical situation.

You are very reluctant to sign a business deal that may enable your company to expand globally. You've got your reasons. A business partner wishes to convince one to sign the agreement because he believes it is well worth it. After trying hard but failing to convince you, he then says something like:

"Imagine what it'd be like when our company grows globally. We'll set up global offices. Other foreign businesses become interested in us. Our popularity and standing will touch the skies, and our market value will increase exponentially.

We are going to earn much more significantly than we are getting now, and we are going to live a five times greater lifestyle than the one we're living now."

These words paint a vibrant picture of your potential success on your mind, you'll probably succumb to the temptation, and you might neglect reason or dismiss the motives that initially compelled you not to sign the offer. Your subconscious mind is immensely more effective than your conscious mind.

[58]

The subconscious mind is where you get to play out all the words your partner has said to you and in clear pictures. You can see your products in use all over the world. You would have imagined traveling a lot and shaking hands over deals. This is the power of the subconscious.

AMBIGUITY

Through ambiguous speeches is the foremost technique, many power-hungry leaders, dictators, and other governmental leaders hypnotize the people. Many so-called excellent political leaders are not anything more than proficient speakers.

Next time there is an election campaign in your region, I would like you to look closely at the sort of words that distinct leaders use to market support and vote.

You will understand that almost all of the time, political leaders' speeches are devoid of logic. They are filled with ambiguity and obscure slogans that serve no other function than to whet the audience's emotions. They are often right because the crowd is always following up with cheers and claps to show their supports.

A logical person uses clear, unambiguous speech and does not wake up the public's emotions, and barely wins an election.

The critical question is: How can you use ambiguous speeches to hypnotize the people? If I make simple, logical, and meaningful statements, your conscious mind finds no issues working out the significance of what I state. For instance:

"Vote for me. I have planned many excellent economic and social policies that are sure to enhance our nation's social and economic requirements. These policies include..."

Sound boring, right?

On the flip side, if I use obscure words and work on instigating your emotions, then it's a huge effect. Your conscious mind is busy figuring out my sentence's logical significance. Meanwhile, I bombard you with ideas to vote for me. For example:

"Great people of Dreamland! I ask you to RISE to the occasion! I ask you to awaken and embrace CHANGE! Together we CAN. This time we chose unity and advancement! This time we are going with Winner's Political Party!";

What challenge am I asking you to grow to? What change am I asking you to adopt?

Your conscious mind becomes busy looking for answers to those unanswerable questions. I toss in the "suggestion"' to vote for me, which immediately reaches your subconscious thoughts. My chances of winning the election out of Dreamland will radically increase.

Ambiguous hypnotic techniques are a common strategy adopted by many in our world today. We see them in use every day by team leaders, motivational speakers, religious leaders. The list goes on.

CONJUNCTIONS

Applying conjunctions is a favorite traditional and covert hypnosis technique. This secret hypnosis technique involves saying a couple of absolute truths initially—something your audience could quickly confirm.

After supplying a string of correct information, you introduce the suggestion that you aspire to program your audiences' minds, connecting it with the remainder of the information with a conjunction such as 'because'.

Consider your subconsciousness to be a club and the Bouncer guarding the club as your conscious mind. The bouncer's responsibility is to guarantee nobody enters the group that has the capability of causing any danger to the individuals inside.

In the same way, the task of your conscious mind would be to keep any information regarding which you might disagree.

At first, the protector is awake and frisks attentively at every individual who enters the bar. In any dialog, we are conscious first once we thoroughly inspect what another person is saying, mainly when he's a stranger.

After the protector checks many individuals and does not find anything suspicious about every one of these, he becomes less careful, exhausted, and idle. He makes his checking less intense.

As we move in dialogue and build trust, we lower our guard. We do not deem it necessary to inspect and examine every word another person utters.

At this phase, a criminal is very likely to take a gun to the bar without being detected due to its bouncer's weariness and nonchalance.

At whatever point you have accumulated trust on a conscious or an oblivious level with a speaker, he additionally gains the ability to program your mind with practically any suggestions he likes.

View the standard speech given by a politician during a political campaign. Visualize yourself as a part of the crowd.

"Ladies and Gentlemen! As I stand here before you tonight in this stunning and enchanting event, I am fairly sure you have gathered with much excitement and enthusiasm.

I feel the same enthusiasm as I'm speaking to you at the moment. You've all gathered here at this amazing event because you trust in our party and our mission."

"Ladies and Gentlemen!" You do not even have to check around to be aware there are gentlemen and ladies around. This announcement, though used to gain attention, is enrolled as truth by your mind.

"As I stand here before you tonight." Obviously, he is standing before you tonight. Another fact and the event is probably a stunning and enchanting one also --yet another reality.

"You've all gathered here..." Without a doubt, you've gathered here and so are filled with enthusiasm --what a futile line to say. Individuals who have assembled to listen to someone talk are usually enthusiastic. The purpose is to tell an evident truth, so you start to trust the speaker.

After building trust, he drops his suggestion: "You trust in our party and our mission."

Notice the way the speaker uses the conjunction "because" to connect two unrelated sentences. You all gather here for this amazing event have nothing to do with you thinking about the speaker's party or mission.

You have come here to be aware of what the party's mission is then to determine for yourself if you need to believe it or not. However, since you've built trust with the speaker, you are very likely to take his suggestion, preceded by a series of absolute truths.

Here Is What the combination "because" does:

At the point when you listen in to the statement, "You have faith in our party and our mission," your mind filters for motivation to accept this assertion. At this stage, you have been mesmerized.

So rather than hunting for a logical reason to think that statement, you take the ridiculous reason the speaker pre-provides, i.e., "You've all gathered here with this superb event."

Before you know it, you're hypnotized and mesmerized by the speaker and vigorously have faith in their mission. It doesn't make a difference.

PRESUPPOSITIONS

Presuppositions are intriguing because, typically, in hypnosis, we distract the conscious mind of someone. After that, we present a suggestion. However, in presupposition, the reverse occurs.

First, we provide the suggestions and then divert the individual's conscious mind to evade its scrutiny.

Let us say I am a salesman with an insurance company seeking to sell you a policy. My objective is to program your mind using the suggestion, "Our policies are distinctive and dependable," you clearly do not believe yet.

If I blurt out, "Our policies are distinctive and dependable." You are not going to believe it right away. Your mind will probably be like, "Oh, really? Why should I believe that? Give me a piece of evidence."

The conscious scrutiny is that we attempt to remove this mindful evaluation in presuppositions, so you take the suggestion without questioning.

So instead, I will rather say to you, "Not only are our policies exceptional and dependable, but they also offer you long-term safety and benefits." Or something similar like, "Apart from our coverages being exceptional and dependable, we also provide you with all sorts of consumer care and support round the clock."

By presupposing my suggestions as an unquestionable fact, I diverted your conscious mind by giving it specific information to consider. Thus, my suggestion is not scrutinized.

Now, you're not likely to question my claim that "our policies are distinctive and dependable." Alternatively, you may ask something like, "What sort of long-term safety and benefits will I get?" Or "What sorts of customer service do you provide?" Or at the very least, "Please tell me more."

ANALOG MARKING

Analog indicating sure seems complicated, but it is something most of us do naturally in discussions. It means highlighting particular keywords and phrases through a dialog. The target is to communicate with an individual's subconscious mind right.

Our subconscious mind always evolves to listen to fluctuations in the environment. This can be known as the oriental reaction.

When you are in an area, and someone passes through the doorway, you turn your head to check who it is. This may look to be a conscious reaction, but the majority of the time, it is not. Most of the time, it is automatic, unconscious, and occurs with no participation of your will.

This conduct response is essential for our genetic legacy. It was useful tens of thousands of years back when people had to shield themselves from predators. At the time, the degree of consciousness of the surroundings changes could have meant the difference between death and life.

Basically, any move in the climate is promptly seen by the subconscious mind. This simple fact is what we use in analog marking. By causing some change from the environment when sending our message through the dialog, we raise the likelihood of communication directly with the individual's subconsciousness.

STEPS TO ANALOG MARKING

First, you need to develop trust and set up compatibility with the individual you are talking with. This may be achieved by stating some details, grinning, seeming friendly, or using a mirroring technique.

Decide ahead what material you need to convey to the individual's unconscious mind. "Something like "Let yourself feel comfortable," because ensuring the individual feels comfortable around you may be extremely beneficial.

Consider an event you will have the option to talk about in which that message you need to send would not be strange. For instance, speaking about a trip to the beach. "I appreciate going to the seashore where you can simply relax and allow yourself to feel comfortable and look at the ocean waves."

At that point, examine the circumstances using a sentence that may adjust the message. "I appreciate going to the seashore where you can simply relax and allow yourself to feel comfortable and look at the ocean waves."

When you get into the embedded message, "let yourself feel comfortable," do something to indicate it out to the individual's unconscious mind to detect. You can do this by lowering your voice's tone, slowing your voice down, touching your arm, lifting your eyebrows, tilting your head, and letting your backrest comfortably on your chair.

Using the descending voice pitch is discovered to be, to some degree, incredible in analog marking.

VOICE TONE

The tone of the voice is a proportion of its shrieks. The more shriek in the voice, the further high-pitched it's believed to be. Think of it as this route for better comprehension. Men typically have low-pitched voices, and ladies ordinarily have piercing voices.

Your voice pitch and tone decide what type of sentence you're saying at a deep subconscious level.

[66]

I recommend you to perform this exercise. I would like you to speak out loud, "What have you done?" in three distinct ways...

First, state it with a high tone where your voice is exhausting and low from the outset. Then it will become sharp and loud toward the end of the sentence. You will observe that the rising pitch becomes processed as a question by our minds. You are asking another person what he's done only out of interest. Additionally, it suggests excitement.

Then, make the statement using a level tone where your voice has a relatively moderate pitch close to the sentence's furthest limit as at the outset. A level toned voice gets process as an assertion by the mind. You likely know precisely what other individual has done and are communicating your disappointment.

In conclusion, say it with a plunging pitch where your voice is boisterous and sharp toward the beginning. At that point, it will turn out to be moderate and low towards the end. A plunging pitched voice gets processed as an order by our mind.

If you did not practice these different vocal pitch levels, you probably would not get the right result, but you will undoubtedly have a better understanding if you do.

As you've observed, the descending pitch opens up the control interface in somebody's mind. People are more disposed to do all that you request them when you talk in a diving pitch as their mind processes it as an order.

HOW TO PERFORM SELF HYPNOSIS

Despite the usual fallacy, a hypnotist can't make you enter a hypnotic state. It is a case of them directing you into this frame of mind. It's actually up to the individual to let themselves enter a trance. It really has very little to do with coercion or willpower, or some other power for that matter.

In reality, it's a testament to a subject if they could enter a hypnotic trance. It's simple to withstand but maybe not relatively as straight forward to enter a trance. Allowing your mind to go to a profound state of relaxation takes some ability on the individual.

Just about everybody can go into a hypnotic trance. On the other hand, the more creative and intelligent people find it the easiest to go to a beautiful, calming, and profoundly relaxing trance state. So those individuals who say things like "you can not hypnotize me" are missing the point. I can't direct anyone to some hypnotic trance who does not wish to go into one. It's all up for them to follow if they want to.

As it's a skill on the subject's part to let themselves enter a hypnotic state, someone could hypnotize themselves with no manual or even a hypnotherapist. This is referred to as self-hypnosis. There are several methods to do so, but this can be one of them.

Get yourself comfortable, either seated or lying down, whichever you want. Close your eyes and take three slow deep breaths.

Count yourself down from 10 to 1 while you relax your whole body. Start from your head and gradually make your way down through the various body parts till you accomplish your feet. Concentrate

[68]

on every place for several moments and focus on that area relaxing before going gradually down to another location. So spend a few minutes focusing on relaxing your mind before going to the neck, then shoulders, etc.

When you have relaxed your entire body, imagine a doorway before you and mentally walk through it. This doorway contributes to a relaxing, calming location. It may be anywhere you choose, like a secluded shore of an enchanting forest. Attempt to use as many senses as possible. Smell the air, listen to some background sounds, and also feel the ground beneath your feet. You are now in a hypnotic state.

During a hypnotic state, you can recite some private affirmations or imagine yourself achieving your objectives. These acts as orders into the subconscious mind, which will always try to accomplish, therefore always be positive. As an example, if you would like to be confident, envision yourself in various scenarios being the positive person you need to be. If you would like to excel at a specific game, then imagine yourself doing exactly that, maybe even winning an award.

Savor this moment for as long as you desire, and attempt to find things as vividly as possible.

When you are done, you can count yourself from this trance. You can achieve so by telling yourself you may feel more alert with every number you count from 1 to 10 till you're completely awake in the count of 10. Then slowly count to 10.

When you open your eyes, observe how calm and relaxed you feel. You may feel somewhat different, in a great way. The experience varies from person to person, but you need to make powerful self-improvements with frequent exercises. You also need to find it a lot easier to enter more profound trance levels as you become more experienced. Like many skills, practice is only going to enhance your ability to do self-hypnosis.

Once you have undergone a guided hypnosis session a couple of times, you will be better placed to direct yourself. You will now understand exactly what the condition of mind you are looking for feels like.

SETTING THE RIGHT MENTAL CONDITION FOR SELF-HYPNOSIS

Possessing a go-to induction system could be helpful since it helps your mind get into the rhythm and get down to the business of the day.

However, naturally, no two days will be the same. What works for you today might be less successful on another, based on your frame of mind. So mixing up things with different methods can be a helpful method to maintain the conscious mind aroused and concentrated before you sink into a deep trance.

However, before beginning with an induction procedure, it's imperative to remind yourself why you would like to enter a trance.

Self-hypnosis is so strong because it allows you to access this subconscious, which explains why it is a wonderful process for tapping into creativity, abundant mindsets, and problem-solving, among several other things.

Having an obvious idea beforehand of what you wish to attain during self-hypnosis will put you off on the perfect foot. However, it's gaining access to the subconscious that frequently poses the best challenge. On the off chance that you are experiencing issues inducing yourself into an entrancing state, don't get disappointed. What you need is patience and more practice to learn.

The subconscious is an element of consciousness that lists every encounter you have ever had, even with people we are not conscious of. Forgotten memories, gut feelings in a circumstance, and even advice outside of your direct experience are available.

It's your subconscious that engineers most of your waking life. Nonetheless, it's more than that. The unconscious possesses an intelligence of its own, and among its significant capacities is to keep you secured.

What is more, your subconscious and conscious minds are regularly communicating together. Therefore by preparing yourself emotionally, you may discover that gaining entry to a subconscious can be readily achieved. In any case, you don't have to accomplish a lot of work; your inner mind will perform the vast majority of it for you.

Educating yourself involves learning how to stop blocking your way, which means you stop preventing yourself from entering a trance. Educating yourself to go into a deep trance involves learning how to let go.

Nevertheless, there are some exercises that you can do to assist with this, and this will also boost your conscious awareness. Since people are inclined to exert a good deal of energy towards restraining problems and unwanted emotions, those exercises might become a crucial part of your practice.

During self-hypnosis, you can divert your energy towards raising your consciousness and finding deeper levels of awareness. To improve your consciousness is to fortify your psychological architecture, which can be accomplished by increasing brain connections, referred to as neural connections.

Among the very best methods for raising the brain, connections are by way of emotions. Specifically, positive emotions construct brain connections. Also, emotions inform you if things are moving wrong or right: they will inform you when you need to go farther inside.

Awareness exercises are best for building a secure mental platform by fostering positive emotions, strengthening your awareness, and raising brain connections.

PREPARING FOR A SUCCESSFUL SELF-HYPNOSIS SESSION

Find a quiet place where you will not be distracted or agitated. Ensure that you're free from the beeps, alarms, and pings of your gadgets. If you need to do something at a particular time, set the alarm. In case you want to listen to guided self-hypnosis audios or audio, shut down the other apps if you are using your laptop.

Select a time of the day or night at which the odds of being bothered are nominal, and you will find it easy to relax. Many people prefer mornings before they begin their daily activities. Others favor doing it before they go to bed. Pick what works best for you. As soon as you have trained yourself to enter a trance readily, you will find it simpler to perform the same through the more challenging times of the day. That may be the precise moment you require self-hypnosis the most. For instance, take time to emotionally prepare yourself before a meeting you are feeling anxious about. However, to start with, but the odds in your favor by picking a pattern that puts you up for success.

Before starting, take a couple of minutes to become mindful of everything you feel and what you would like to attain while practicing self-hypnosis. Are you feeling anxious or concerned about the moment, or tired? Are you feeling rested? Precisely what do you need to achieve? Clarity, comfort, focus? Knowing these things before you begin can allow you to acknowledge any possible roadblocks and establish a definite intention for your practice.

As soon as you have established the ideal physical and mental space for your self-hypnosis exercise, you are prepared to experiment together with the induction procedures, visualization methods, and mindfulness exercises previously mentioned.

As soon as you have established the ideal physical and mental space for your self-hypnosis exercise, you are prepared to experiment together with the induction procedures, visualization methods, and mindfulness exercises previously mentioned.

DARK HYPNOSIS

THE DARK SIDE OF HYPNOSIS

Hypnosis is clear access to the mind, where the hypnotherapist to the hypnotist has a pathway to the subject's mind. This access may be used to harm in addition to good, both unintentionally and intentionally. Here some risks that practitioners, therapists, and even clients who make themselves available, should be aware of.

TAKING AWAY THE SENSE OF WILLINGNESS

We are aware that feeling a feeling of control over our lives is an inherent human desire. It's not up to therapists to make assumptions about client requirements. Therefore, it's crucial that any modifications a client is guided to create, having been inducted into a trance state, are subsequent goals established ahead of and clearly understood by both the client and therapist.

It is also essential to provide our clients with the resources to manage themselves independently and as swiftly as possible. Therefore, therapists will need to learn effective short methods and teach the client to relax rather than rely on guided imagery delivered by people or on tapes provided to them.

MUDDIED OBJECTIVE

The intention of this therapist bringing the intervention is hugely significant when it comes to the final results. If there's sincere intent to assist an individual, even a therapist who is not technically skillful can arrive at a fantastic outcome.

Ego can pose a specific difficulty for many who use hypnotherapy since they have found it is simple to place people into a trance. Whereas, to many, it appears a mysterious procedure. They may also have persuaded themselves that it takes immense ability and particular rascality involving arm levitation and so forth. So their egos puff up, and that's hugely damaging for patients. This is why it is recommended that professionals use the expression guided imagery instead of hypnosis to stop misconceptions about both therapist and client.

Luckily, one of our inherent sources, which can complement the concentrated trance country, is "observing self." On a biological level, this consciousness occurs when we relax. The cerebrum may function without intense psychological interference, allowing us to look in reality more logically and comprehend when we are too carried away with ourselves.

CREATING ILLUSORY MEMORIES

The simplicity by which false memory can be achieved has been shown countless times, primarily through psychologist Elizabeth Loftus's pioneering work. From the 1980s and 1990s, families have torn apart because of presumed recollections of parental sexual maltreatment being "revealed" during treatment.

In one of its first significant conferences, the European Therapy Studies Institute alerted practitioners of illusory recollection syndrome. In one instance, a young lady remembered in therapy that she was repeatedly raped by Satanists, including relatives and other people in the neighborhood. However, it appeared later that she was only conversing with her therapists.

So therapists will need to be careful not to create emotionally arousing ideas, even in queries. For example, about the potential for childhood abuse or neglect or that a spouse might be having an affair which a client may then latch on to and later dream about, then remember the dream and give credence to it, without any firm evidence to back it up in the real world.

INDUCING HALLUCINATIONS,

Inducing delusions can lead susceptible individuals into uncontrollable breakdowns. This is very common among stage hypnotists. It is dangerous as an individual hallucinating cannot differentiate between the dream state and waking reality in the manner that we generally do.

CONDITIONING

Cults and political parties practice hypnosis consciously or unconsciously. For instance, the usage by politicians of abstract hypnotic words such as "positive shift," "values," or "principles" induces people into the subconscious to look for what they know as the significance of those words. However, politicians provide no concrete illustrations. Everybody wants to change something in their lives. Nobody wants a negative change. So when a politician uses change, transformation, or innovation, it's nothing but a con trick.

Anyone who believes hypnosis is benign might be wise to keep in mind that Hitler studied it after being treated by a hypnotist of this hysterical blindness he endured after the First World War. His character changed because of a strong suggestion in a trance state by a psychologist who informed him he was unique and had excellent personal abilities. He suggested to him that with these powers, he could heal himself of blindness. This acted as a post-hypnotic suggestion, and Hitler proceeded to induce receptive trance states in enormous crowds at rallies, bombarding them with emotionally stimulating nominalizations. He adopted a stylized kind of arm levitation as the Nazi salute.

Obviously, in treatment, abstract terminology is used with kind goals to deliver clients in their internal research to find significance for internal resources, imagination, and strengths. However, it's vital to remain mindful of how power can easily be abused and unintended impacts when speech is used broadly.

At the minimum, the over-use of all trance-inducing favorable concepts can prevent a subject from moving ahead if specific concepts are not made concrete. For example, assume that a client scales herself in a two for depression on a scale in which one is the deepest of depressions and ten is alive being again.

The therapist then asks what amount of this scale the client will have to feel fulfilled. The customer says 8 or 7. We all have a pair of abstracts, such as the descriptors for 1 and 10 and a few meaningless numbers over mid-scale.

Unless the therapist ascertains that the client's behavior is 1 and 10 and 7 or 8, the client has nothing tangible to work together to create positive changes. Also, the therapist has nothing for the client to rehearse in guided imagery. Always follow with questions like, "What does it look like?"

When clients talk in abstract terms, occasionally therapists themselves become jaded from the abstractions, go in their inner hunts, and don't see beyond them. The point is it can be effortless to be seduced into a trance, even once you believe you understand better.

DAMAGING AN INDIVIDUAL'S ESSENCE

Hypnotic techniques help individuals access a state of a deeper subconscious. We tap into that person's unique substance that life induces programmed into them at conception, which then expects certain influences, as a spark expects wind for it to fan into flame. So it might grow and grow and consequently continue the evolutionary procedure.

The hypnotic induction is, in actuality, a kind of trespass upon the personal mental territory of the essence. We should enter this state if encouraged in, and we have to take care to shut the gate correctly if we leave. Utilizing hypnosis repeatedly with an individual is ultimately depriving them since it can put the flicker of willingness by making them more open to suggestion, rather than just to the hints of their therapist. That's an important reason why hypnotherapy sessions should be as brief as possible.

Therapy aims to assist people in detaching and dealing, not become reliant. Intense hypnosis instances can even finally derange the

[78]

mind, as ordinary people begin behaving in gruesome manners and think of others as lesser people and 'things.'

When the self-righteous behead people who do not share their faith or think it's okay to rape, kill and torture people, they have been hypnotized with psychological arousal usage through fear, chanting, repetition, promises, or other ways, to make them highly suggestible. Most deadly mass movements involve entrancing and the programming of people when they are mentally stimulated.

A variant may occur if therapists try to reinforce a mentally damaged person by telling them that they are gifted, desired, or have a fantastic future ahead, backed with no evidence, and doing something tangible to make this a reality. Reckless use of hypnosis can disrupt a person's spiritual and mental growth.

When we think of mind control, many people picture the regular school bully once we think about a commanding individual. We might envision somebody who aggressively orders the others to do precisely what they need.

In real sense, mind control is a means of subverting psychological techniques to control an individual's thoughts, behavior, emotions, feelings, or decisions. One recognized method used to achieve this is hypnosis.

Mind control identifies a procedure where a team or person systematically uses unethically manipulative methods to convince other people to adapt to the manipulator's wishes. These wishes are often to the detriment of the exploited individual. The term refers to any technique, passionate or something else, which might be considered sabotaging somebody's inclination of authority over their reasoning, conduct, feelings, or decisions.

Theories of brainwashing and mind control were initially designed to describe how totalitarian regimes seemed to indoctrinate prisoners of war via torture and propaganda methodically. These concepts were later enlarged and altered by psychologists to describe a broader selection of phenomena, particularly conversions to new spiritual movements.

A third-generation concept is centered on the use of mind control to keep members of religions and cults. The proposal that religions use mind control methods has caused legal and scientific controversy.

YOUR MIND IS ALREADY BEING CONTROLLED

Your mind has been controlled by remote strangers that do not have your best interests in mind. It appears to be a delusion. These are the findings of a collection of scientific studies that reveal how several dominant associations can influence how you feel and how you behave. The ideal approach to cast a ballot without you genuinely think about it.

Intentional mind control of the majority is, is nothing new. Almost a century ago, our worldwide mania for consumption had been unleashed with insights to the subconscious to develop new thought control methods to make the modern American customer.

There was a necessity to shift America from a "need" to a "desire" society. Individuals have to be educated to desire new things before the older have been completely consumed. A new mentality has been shaped. An Individual's desires must overshadow his needs.

Back in 1928, Edward Bernays, portrayed as the "Father of Public Relations," gladly clarified how his strategies for mental control had permitted a little elite to control the minds of the American public.

The conscious and creative manipulation of the masses' coordinated behavior and feelings is a significant component in a democratic society. The individuals who control this concealed society establish an imperceptible government that is the nation's are real ruling power.

We are represented, our minds shaped, our preferences framed, our thoughts proposed, to a great extent by men we have never known before. In pretty much every demonstration of our daily lives, we are overwhelmed by the moderately modest number of people who pull the wires that control the public mind.

Bernays started a movement that we have all understood as a vital part of our capitalist ecosystem. Mass media usage to market roles, needs, and status symbols that pours in profit for businesses.

The frightening expressions of Wayne Chilicki, CEO of General Mills, uncover how dependably Bernays' vision was followed. "With regards to focusing on youngster clients, we at General Mills follow the Procter & Gamble version support to the grave. "We have confidence in getting them early and having them forever."

The progressions we are seeing are another generation of mind controllers using the advancing technology of information mining and web-based media to infuse their control considerably more

[81]

profound into our heads than their progenitors may have envisioned conceivable.

A current Bernays called B.J. Fogg had set an order called "captology," gotten from the abbreviation CAPT or "Computers Persuasive Technology." He instructs new graduates on the most proficient method to utilize innovation to "change individuals' perspectives or attitudes."

His teachings have bred the ports of our newest everyday routines. The chimes from our smartphones distract us, the thumbs-up icon on the news feeds, and the Like numbers telling us how accepted we are.

These are "hot triggers" that kick off behavioral circles within our subconscious. Robust programming that instructs us are the ones that activate a temporary need, then provide us with an immediate solution. The remedy sparks a microdose of endorphins within our brains. That feels great. Therefore, like rats on a wheel, we all find ourselves becoming hooked, heading back to get more.

Facebook has built its worldwide reign of 2 billion dynamic clients on this addictive daily schedule. Facebook's key trigger is FOMO: Fear Of Missing Out. People advanced in agrarian groups, where endurance implied being important for the network. The social nervousness of missing what our companions are doing emerges from profound inside our hormonal framework.

Then, Some analysts have brought up that we sacrifice our everyday closeness with people around us by concentrating on the screen in our grasp.

Facebook has been experimenting with the degree of its control over our conduct, manipulating its clients as test subjects. On the final voting day in 2010, it sent "Go out and vote" suggestions to more than 60 million clients, causing an expected 340,000 to cast a ballot who in any case would not have.

Imagine if it decided to send these suggestions to a specific party or a particular candidate's supporters. It could undoubtedly flip a political decision without anybody thinking about it. Under current law, it would not need to mention to anybody what it was doing. In another examination, which caused a public objection, Facebook effectively controlled the emotional condition of 689,000 clients by sending them either an abundance of positive or negative terms in their news feeds.

Social media is not where mind control ends. Do you have trust in your independence when you're cautiously exploring a keyword and using Google to look for something? Reconsider. Therapist Robert Epstein has uncovered the enormous subconscious intensity of what he's known as the Search Engine Manipulation Effect or SEME.

This impact depends on the way we search. We click a fraction of the time on one of the initial two outcomes. Over 90% of our clicks are on the primary ten links presented on the first page of a Google search. There may be a vast number of other web pages containing our keywords. However, Google chooses which ones we will peruse.

Epstein and his partner Ronald Robertson needed to test whether SEME could affect how individuals chose to cast a ballot in a political decision. They requested a sample from Americans to explore contenders for an Australian election using their own fake web search engine, "Kadoodle." They haphazardly separated the example "citizens" into three groups and presented similar outcomes to each.

The primary difference is in the way the results were arranged. One set of individuals backed one candidate. Another set supported the opposition, and the last set saw results showing support for none of the candidates.

The outcomes were faltering. The extent of individuals preferring Kadoodle's "supported" candidate expanded by 48%. Shockingly, 3/4 of individuals in the controlled set were uninformed of any predisposition in their search results. In the "impartial" control set, there was no massive change in opinion.

They've recreated these discoveries in more significant tests led across the United States from that point forward. They've found that using straightforward techniques can cover the manipulation, so nobody knows they see one-sided rankings. In 2014, they took their testing to India during the political race for Prime Minister, where individuals were too acquainted with the candidates. They had the option to move the proportion of individuals preferring a picked candidate by 20%, with 99.5% of individuals indicating no awareness they were being controlled.

In numerous nations of the world, including the U.S., Google has close syndication over web searches. The search-ranking business is entirely unregulated, and courts have decided that Google's entitlement to rank list items, anyway it satisfies, is secured as a type of free discourse. On the off chance that Google chose to swing the U.S. political decision, they could likely do as such without anybody knowing about it.

Hillary Clinton once recruited a long-time Google boss as her chief technology officer. Did Google ever appear supportive of Hillary and promoted pro-Hilary search listings over those preferring Bernie Sanders or later Donald Trump? We may never know.

The British financial analyst Kenneth Boulding once cautioned: "A universe of inconspicuous autocracy is possible, actually utilizing the types of democratic government." So you choose, is your mind being controlled?

There are a few things we can do pending when these inconspicuous influencers are better regulated. One thought, recommended by technology thought pioneer Jaron Lanier, is to research your relationship with social media and reclaim your capacity to pick by carrying out your analyses.

Deliberately experience times of complete separation from social media, like a day, week, or a month, and observe how it feels. How did you feel, and how many times did you fight the desire to reconnect to social media? Let's evaluate further. Did you miss anything? Was there anything positive that replaced the attachment to social media?

Another thought is to get mindful of the origins of our news. Notice the degree to which you live in a data storehouse. Make it a habit of checking the sites of information sources outside your ideological safe place.

When directing an inquiry on Google, see what's recorded a few pages down, and infrequently attempt an alternative internet searcher for a rude awakening.

We can utilize the knowledge that our minds are being controlled to dig further into the model of thought imparted in us from early childhood stages by our way of life.

What thoughts do we underestimate that are truly developments of the worldwide corporate benefit machine? What certain convictions do we hold about the world that are only the consequence of profound social teaching?

While intentionally looking for implying examples that could prompt a more fair and sustainable world, Posing these inquiries offers a pathway of freedom from the mind control those far off outsiders are endeavoring to force on us.

BE CONSCIOUS OF THESE MIND CONTROL TECHNIQUES

For broader and easier identification of what mind control is, let us look at more simple techniques used by regular people in interpersonal relationships and groups.

ALIENATION

Physical isolation can be quite strong. However, even if physical separation is impossible or not functional, manipulators will generally try to alienate you psychologically. This could be accomplished in many ways, from one-week conventions from the country to condemning your loved ones and inner circle. Limiting any distracting influence by controlling information flow is the primary goal.

SOCIAL PROOF AND PEER PRESSURE

Individuals who try to control a vast gathering will typically utilize peer pressure and social proof to program newbies. Social proof is a psychological occurrence in which a group of people assumes that others' beliefs and actions are proper. Since everyone does something, it must be appropriate.

This works particularly well when an individual is unsure of what to believe, how to act, or what to do. Many people in these situations tend to follow what others do as a validation for what they will do.

CRITICISM

Criticism might be utilized as an isolation instrument. The manipulators will typically use an "us versus them" language to criticize the external forces and maintain their excellence. Trying to portray a sense of you has to feel blessed to be connected to them all along.

REPETITION

Constant repetition is just another useful persuasion tool. Even though it might seem overly simplistic to work, repeating the same message continuously makes it comfortable and easier to recall. When repetition is coupled with social proof, it drives the message home clear without any form of ambiguity.

The occurrence of affirmations as a self-explanatory technique is just another evidence that repeating something is useful. If you can convince yourself via repetition, odds are someone may try to use repetition to control you into believing and acting in a particular way.

FEAR OF LONELINESS

New arrivals to a manipulative group will typically first get a receptive welcome. They will form new and deeper friendships that may seem passionate and more closely knitted than any previous ones. Later on, if any doubts arise, these associations will develop into a powerful instrument to maintain them from your group. Even if they are not entirely convinced, life in the external world might appear very lonely.

WEAKNESS

Exhaustion and lack of sleep bring about physical and mental sluggishness. At the point when you are genuinely drained and less ready, you are more helpless to persuasion. A study mentioned in the Journal of Experimental Psychology shows that people who had not slept for just 21 hours were more vulnerable to suggestions.

IDENTITY CRISES

Eventually, the manipulators intend to reshape your identity. They would like you to stop being yourself and become a robot, someone who follows their orders. Employing all of the methods and mind manipulation methods mentioned previously will extract a confession from you. Some type of recognition that you think they are good people doing a fantastic thing.

Initially, it may be insignificant, like agreeing that group members are loving and fun people or legitimate perspectives. As soon as you accept this one small thing, you might be more prepared to take a different one and then another one and yet another.

Before you know it, from a need to be consistent with everything you say and do, you get started identifying as among the bunch. This is especially powerful if you know your confessions were filmed or recorded. Just in case you forget, there's physical evidence of your new identity.

At this point, take a little time out to ponder on the groups you belong to, either online or offline. Are they manipulating you?

Hypothetically speaking, let assume you joined "World Peace." Everything began with a little donation, then some fun occasion with many new friends. Before you know it, you're invading the Capitol protesting the validation of electoral results. At the same time, your livelihood and education are placed on hold. What happened? Can you claim World Peace manipulated you into doing so? No.

They influenced you. While they made you do something you'd never think about doing, WorldPeace did not use you to their benefit. They asked you to do exactly what they feel is appropriate, and you consented. They have no personal gain here.

Compare this to a commanding karate teacher, who's verbally and emotionally abusive toward his protegee while expecting total respect and obedience in return. He makes them believe that they are the only group of individuals who are just about to unravel some peculiar secret, making both Terminator and Rambo look small.

Whether his motives are monetary or a simple desire to restrain and feel exceptional, there's absolutely no doubt he's utilizing the mind manipulation methods mentioned previously.

Matters get even more complicated when you find that your spouse is exploiting you.

CHARACTER TRAITS OF CONTROLLING PEOPLE

Suppose you have ever felt like something is wrong, especially with you, in a cozy relationship or casual experience. For example, you feel you are being pressured, commanded, or maybe feel as though you are questioning yourself frequently more than usual. It might be manipulation.

Manipulation is a genuinely undesirable mental methodology used by people who cannot request what they want directly. Individuals that are attempting to manipulate others are trying to restrain them.

There are several kinds of manipulation range from a forceful salesperson to an emotionally abusive partner. Some of these behaviors are easier to identify than others.

Explained here are signs you might be the subject of manipulation.

YOU ARE ALWAYS AT FAULT

People who like to control or manipulate your mind never take responsibility for anything. They tend to blame you for minor things even when it has nothing to do with you. They simply take on the role of victim and force you to think you are responsible for matters beyond your control.

You may hear some like "it is all your fault" or "you should not have." Even when they assault or abuse you, they will use words like, "You made me do this." In most cases, you end up feeling sorry and believe you are responsible as the person has made you believe.

CONSTANT CRITICISM

A controlling person will try to weaken your confidence by creating using words that make fun of you or kills your self-esteem in the public or private space.

Listed below are a couple of examples of those techniques used to control your mind:

- They are always exaggerating your imperfections at work, in the house, or anywhere by continually pointing out typos in an email, how you dressed, walked to talk.

- They never praise you for doing something appropriate.

- They become overly mad if you do not answer your phone on time.

- They make sensitive jokes about you in public, not minding how you feel.

THEY WANT TO OWN YOU

Their primary mind control technique is that they always demand attention and slowly isolate you from friends and family. They will attempt to keep you all to themselves by whining about how frequently you hang out with certain friends or relatives.

It is not always evident. They could glare at you when you are on the phone with somebody, talk to another person in public or at a party, or groan if you go to spend some time with family.

THEY KEEP SCORE

For the most part, they anticipate something and cause you to feel contrite if you don't do what they need. They track every nice gesture.

When they pay for your dinner on a date or allow you to sleepover at their place, for instance, they will bring this up repeatedly. They may likewise make a special effort to appear to be too liberal as a way to keep you obliged to them.

THEY GASLIGHT YOU

They underplay your expertise by bending or depriving you of being too sensitive. If you are upset about something that they told you a week ago, they will deny ever having mentioned it, and it's all on your mind. You begin second-guessing yourself all the time.

When you complain of a mutual friend spreading fake news about you, in response, they will make you feel like you imagine things that never happened or blame it on someone else, irrespective of the clearing evidence.

THEY ARE DRAMATIC

When you get a big break or win a pitch at work, and everyone is celebrating you. A controlling person will find a way to change the topic by brooding over something about them to transfer attention back to themselves.

They may likewise sabotage your relationships with others as a way to have a significant advantage over you. For instance, they may take screenshots of your personal texts without consent and send them to other people or break unpleasant news about you to other people when you are not ready.

THEY APPLY SCARE TACTICS

They are control freaks at work or in a relationship who like to show off as your superiors even when they are not. At work, this may appear in the form of a co-worker who continually interrupts you at a meeting to express their view or even a boss that scornfully talks down at you in front of your coworkers. It could be a partner who will not let you have a say on any matter in a relationship. They even go as far as deciding what to wear and your meal when on a date.

In some cases, they employ threats in the form of a joke by saying something like, "I will break up with you if" or "If you do not turn this in by tomorrow, I'll begin clearing your desk out." They will claim they want you to be a better person.

THEY EXHIBIT CONSTANT MOOD SWINGS

You can never predict what mood you will get when it comes to these types of mind controllers. They switch moods within seconds. They exhibit intense mood swings. One minute they are buying you presents and lavishes you with compliments, and the next, they act like a bully.

[93]

You wind up feeling as if you are walking on eggshells and never know where you stand with people like this. Additionally, they will not take responsibility or apologizing when they are upset with you.

UNHEALTHY JEALOUSY

Controlling people always want you to focus on them at all times. They want your undivided attention anywhere, anytime. Some of the patterns these type of people display include;

Making unsavory comments about you or your friends

Interrogate you about where you are going and the person you are going to be with

They are unhappy whenever you meet someone new and plan to hang out with them.

THEY DON'T TAKE, "NO."

A controlling individual often will not take "NO" for an answer. They will attempt to convince or pressure you to change your mind. You can see this in the form of stalking. Even after a relationship has been called off, a controlling person still wants to interfere with the other persons by continually sabotaging their relationships and following them everywhere they go.

If you have said, you can not meet up this weekend. Then they will appear uninvited to your home. Or they will refuse to allow you to leave a party early after stating you are feeling ill.

THEY WANT YOU TO CHANGE

It's all about them, and they want you to transform to suit their selfish interest. They are constantly pressuring you to dress in a certain way, choosing your words for you if you ever get to speak. They can lock you in and prevent you from going out until you dress in a certain way or wear a particular outfit.

GASLIGHTING AS A FORM OF MIND CONTROL

Gaslighting is common in relationships. It's an emotionally abusive relationship found among couples. This is an act of manipulation that forces the other partner in the relationship to question everything about them. A victim of gaslighting could be pushed far to the point that they question their mental stability. The manipulator makes them doubt their memories, thoughts, and the events around them.

The expression "Gaslighting" started from a film called "Gaslight." In this movie, the husband was abusive towards his wife to the extent where she questions her sanity and entire existence. She was convinced she was going crazy.

Gaslighting, either deliberate or not, is a sort of manipulative control. Gaslighting can occur in various relationships, such as supervisors, bosses, friends, and even parents. However, among the most devastating kinds of gaslighting is the relationship between husband and wife.

HOW TO IDENTIFY GASLIGHTING

Gaslighting is a severe psychological challenge, especially if the victim is unaware they are being manipulated. Gaslighting occurs in personal relationships, and in rare cases, in professional relationships. A manipulative boss or colleague is going after a subordinate, and even by well-known individuals. It's important to note that this sort of manipulative control can also occur between parents and their children.

Here are some signs to help you identify if you are a victim of gaslighting.

- When you can no longer make decisions yourself
- Feeling alienated from family and friends.
- You blame yourself for your partner's abusive behavior towards you.
- You hide information from family and friends about your relationship with your spouse because you don't want to be confronted.
- Lost of enthusiasm towards life and all outdoor activities you use to enjoy
- Feeling uncomfortable all the time but unable to identify why
- Wondering if you were unreasonable or not loving enough by questioning if your reaction to your spouse is proper
- You apologize for everything and on behalf of everyone.
- Always believing it Is your fault If things go wrong.
- You are frequently wondering if you Are overly sensitive.
- Feeling like everything you do is wrong.

- Wondering if you are too sensitive about issues
- No More feeling like the person you were
- Being more stressed and less confident than you were

EXAMPLES OF GASLIGHTING

Individuals who use gaslighting to manipulate others are professionals at pushing the buttons of their victims. They know how susceptible and weak you are and use it against you, mostly in an abusive way. People like this make you doubt your decisions, question your memory, and doubt yourself. Examples of gaslighting include

Belittling your feelings

"You cry too much,"

"Really! Now you want to start feeling emotional over this?"

Convincing you about other people

"Everyone thinks you did a terrible job."

"The whole office thinks you've lost your touch."

They deny what previous conversations.

"No, I never said anything like that. You must have misunderstood my word."

"I never said I would pick our daughter from school. What are you saying? Now, she's going to be alone in the class after all the other kids have left."

They hide objects from you.

"You really can't find the car keys. Where did you drop it last night?"

"I'm surprised you can't find a jacket. Why do you do this all the time?"

Insist you were not at a place where you were

"I know you will never come through for me. You couldn't show up at our Christmas party."

"I'm really disappointed. You failed to show up for our kids."

ESCAPING GASLIGHTING

Getting out of a gaslighting situation can be painfully difficult. Nonetheless, it's possible. The solution to gaslighting is higher psychological awareness and self-regulation—both in knowledge and in action.

Employing these emotional abilities, the victim learns they don't need anyone to confirm their reality. They are, therefore, building self-reliance and confidence in establishing their particular reality. They'll also understand it is possible to handle these uneasy feelings of standing within their certainty in resistance to a gaslighter. This may be particularly challenging if the person is a victim of abuse and needs a substantial change in mindset and abilities during treatment.

Here are some proven measures that have helped patients in recent time

Describe the issue.

Recognizing the challenge is the very initial step. Name what's happening between you and your partner, friend, family member, colleague, or boss.

Separate the facts from aberrations.

Document all your dialog in a diary so that you may have an objective look at it. Where's the dialogue turning away from reality in the other person's view? Then after you examine the dialog, write down how you felt. Start looking for indicators of repeated refusal of your experience.

Check to confirm power tussle with your spouse.

Should you discover yourself having the same conversation over and over again and can not appear to convince them to admit your perspective, you may be getting gaslighted.

Carry our mental exercises to support a shift in mindset.

Picture yourself outside the relationship or continuing it for a considerable time in the future. Critically, cast the vision in a good light, regardless of whether it makes you feel uneasy. Think not far off when you will have your existence, social help, and integrity.

Be willing to give up something.

Part of what makes it painful and hard to depart a gaslighting relationship is that gaslighter could be a "person" you have committed to. For example, someone like your wife, husband, best friend, mother, sister, or brother. It is fine to walk away from toxicity, wherever it's coming from.

[99]

Allow yourself to feel all of your feelings.

Accept and admit what you believe is right. I suggest monitoring your feelings. Think about trying a Mood Meter app. It is a simple way to ease the understanding of your emotions and monitor your routines. This will enable you to understand what causes your emotions and provides helpful plans to change your moods.

Speak with your real friends.

Inquire from them if you look like yourself and check on your partner's behavior. Ask them to be objectively honest.

Concentrate on how you feel rather than wrong and right.

It's anything but difficult to become involved with the need to be right or spend endless hours ruminating about who is correct. However, determining who's wrong and right is not as important as how you are feeling. Should your dialogue leaves you feeling awful or second-guessing yourself, that is precisely what you want to look closely at. Having mental and emotional sanity in a relationship is substantially more significant than being off-base or right always.

You can only control your position even when you are right.

You may not ever get your partner or your boss or friend to agree you are not overly sensitive or too controlling or anything else. It'd be best you let go of attempting, as bothersome as this is. The only individual whose assessment you can handle is yours.

Have compassion on your own.

This is truly hard, in any event, when you are not in a compromising dynamic. However, when you're not feeling confident and assertive,

[100]

it is even more challenging to give yourself the benefit of the doubt, love, and kindness. It will be a mending impact and help you push ahead in your decision making.

RECOGNIZING CONTROLLING PEOPLE

It is probably your friend/spouse/boss/partner who is a great individual: Why would they attempt to control you?

There are a couple of explanations for controlling behavior that may clarify why an Individual wants to keep control over a circumstance, or in this case, somebody else:

INSECURITY

Controlling behavior is frequently caused by fear or unhappiness on the controller's part, regardless of the image of confidence and strength he or she often puts up.

HIGH-FUNCTIONING STRESS

Everything may seem on the exterior to be the peak of organization, preparedness, or leadership. They seem to have the whole day planned to the last second. These could be the indicators of high-functioning anxiety. They can use control as a coping mechanism to make security for their spiraling concerns and anxieties. Being the one accountable is great for them, allowing them control over the small information.

LOW SELF-ESTEEM

Counterintuitively, a commanding individual might also have severe problems with low-esteem. Perhaps he or she had been given up as a kid or experienced any other type of lasting abuse. They can not think anyone would genuinely care for them, so they attempt to control or "buy love."

OBSESSIVE-COMPULSIVE PERSONALITY DISORDER - OCPD

Even without a bad self-image or previous trauma, individuals who control one part of your life may be subconsciously compensating for insufficient control in another. In extreme instances, the controller may even be suffering from OCPD.

According to psychologists, the clinical term for this condition is Obsessive-Compulsive Personality Disorder (OCPD). Individuals with this sort of disorder consistently imagine that they know better than the other person. In this manner, in any event, when they are doing something incorrectly, they believe they are correct because it is tough for a control freak to acknowledge that the individual can likewise not be right.

Knowing where controlling behavior comes from does not make it any less frustrating, particularly if the controller is a friend or loved one you do not want to cut off from.

SIGNS YOUR PARTNER IS MIND CONTROLLING, TOXIC, AND POSSIBLY DANGEROUS

Danger signs in relationships might be simple to overlook or easy to dismiss. However, if you believe there may be indications your spouse is controlling, you should be on high alert. The more involved you get with a commanding spouse, the deeper your emotional connection and the lower your strength to fight their suppression. The harder it will be to escape a potentially harmful situation. Somebody who attempts to mind control you is also able to act manipulatively.

They could attempt to convince you that their needs are for your good and the relationship's benefit. When they are around your loved ones and friends, they are on their very best behavior, but they might try to gaslight you privately.

There are warnings that you ought to be suspicious of. Individually, all those signs do not necessarily imply that you are in a hazardous relationship. However, if you recognize at least more than one of those red flags in your relationship, reach out to friends, loved ones, or even a mental health professional immediately.

THEY ARE UNHAPPY WHEN YOU MAKE PLANS WITHOUT THEM

If your life partner regularly gets baffled once you make arrangements that exclude them, that can cause concern. Moreover, if you do wander out without them, a toxic partner may text and call you. On the off chance that your life partner can not allow you to live in life outside your relationship, they probably don't trust you.

This behavior is particularly worrying when they get angry if you don't check in with them or refuse to use place trackers to keep track of your movement. This may show a desire to monitor your activity all the time.

THEY SNOOP THROUGH YOUR PHONE AND YOUR ITEMS

If your spouse ever snoops through your possessions with no approval, it's a clear breach of your privacy, private space, and trust.

Someone who does not respect your space is somebody who does not respect you or your boundaries.

THEY MAKE YOU FEEL BAD ABOUT SPENDING TIME WITH OTHERS

Even if your spouse encourages you to hang out with your family and friends, their behavior can be commanding. They can act intentionally, guilting you into feeling terrible about it once you get home. That is toxic behavior. Any belittling queries or taunts may be a sign they are not in agreement with it.

Ideally, your spouse should encourage you to get a life outside of your relationship. Should they try to keep you inside the boundaries of your partnership, that is a significant red flag.

THEY TALK IN DIRECTIVES OR COMMANDS

If each sentence your spouse says to you seems like it ends with an exclamation point, they might not see you as their equivalent. Furthermore, take note of signs of condescension or contempt in your discussions, which might suggest that they're intentionally attempting to belittle you, a very toxic behavior.

THEY THREATEN TO HURT THEMSELVES OR YOU FOR FAILING TO DO THEIR DESIRE

Anybody who threatens violence does not care about your psychological, emotional, or physical well-being. This behavior is both physically and emotionally abusive. It shows your spouse is prepared to do anything required to bend you and make sure things move their way.

THEY CONSTANTLY SHOW SIGNS OF INSECURITY

If your spouse always seems sure you're cheating on them without incitement or signs, that is just another red flag. While they may be combating their insecurities or have been influenced by adultery in previous relationships, it is unfair for them always to question your devotion to the relationship with no actual reason to do so.

THEY ALWAYS REQUEST SOMETHING OF YOU AS A PROVE TO SHOW YOUR LOVE FOR THEM

If your spouse has a tradition of asking you to demonstrate your love for them by, for instance, cutting off friends and family from your life. In some cases, they ask you to move in with them before you are ready for such a big decision. They might be more interested in their capacity to control you than they're in your real dedication and love for them. In reality, they might be testing your limitations while their needs become more and more frustrating.

THEY WEIRDLY SURPRISE YOU; ONCE YOU STEP OUT OR TRAVELING WITHOUT THEM

A spouse who surprises you with a bouquet at the end of a very long day is entirely different from one who shows up for a family vacation or ladies' night unannounced. If your spouse frequently makes unwarranted expansive gestures, they might use love as a bad disguised excuse to check up on you when you are least expecting it.

THEY CRITICIZE YOU CONSISTENTLY

If your spouse always seems to have something negative to say about your clothing, the best way to spend your own time, or who you hang out with. They may not have your welfare at heart. Instead, this strategy may function as an intentional, continuous reminder you won't ever be great enough. In cases like this, their principal objective is that you begin to doubt yourself too.

BRAINWASHING

WHAT IS BRAINWASHING

It's highly improbable that you're an object of intentional brainwashing. You are presumably dependent upon some of the regular procedures associated with the not precisely moral practice. It is a sort of great control.

We often relate the training with cult groups and don't consider its reality in our regular daily existence. In any case, Brainwashing strategies are frequently used by publicists, news programs, government policies, and numerous others.

Wikipedia defines brainwashing as

Mind control (also known as brainwashing, coercive persuasion, mind abuse, thought control, or thought reform) refers to a process in which a group or individual "systematically uses unethically manipulative methods to persuade others to conform to the wishes of the manipulator(s), often to the detriment of the person being manipulated."

Brainwashing occurs in our everyday life, whether we are conscious of it or not. It doesn't take ancient spells, fancy tools, or hypnotism to brainwash people. Political leaders and the media are examples of forces that are continually brainwashing us. All you need to do is take an in-depth look at everything around you, on social media, religious gatherings, and the world at large.

This form of manipulation happens when an external influence, usually an individual or group of individuals, systematically controls another individual or group of individuals to conform to the ideas and thoughts of the "brainwashed." This can be accomplished by manipulating your mind through procedures that it generally uses for learning and information reception.

The entire procedure is performed over a prolonged time. It is a gradual process in most cases. Basically, you are being molded at the neurological level to get your manipulator's input and think it is your thought. Does this sound familiar?

The primary purpose of brainwashing is to reprogram your thoughts to produce a particular type of reaction.

PRECONDITIONS FOR BRAINWASHING INCLUDE

- Confident temperament
- An average level of intelligence
- Someone to try the techniques on

DOES BRAINWASHING WORK?

How do brainwashing work in psychology and our daily lives, what exactly is brainwashing, and what is the process of brainwashing a person?

While the Korean war was ongoing, the American hostages held in the prison yards were allegedly brainwashed by the Korean and

Chinese. A lot of captives confessed under duress to waging germ warfare. They were forced to vow their loyalty to communism at the end of their captivities. Many soldiers refused to return to their home (United States) after finishing their term.

Psychology defined the study of brainwashing as "Thought Reformation." This falls within the range of "social influence." Social influence takes place every second of the day. This is the diversity of ways another individual is deleting other people's personal opinions, convictions, attitudes, or responses to the outside world. Most times, this is done through a compliance procedure or Luring.

The compliance process often comes as a command. It does not aim at the attitude or conviction. Instead, it is directed at the behavior of the victim. Luring or persuasion, however, takes care of the conviction and attitude. It often comes with the dangled benefit. For example, you will be more wealthy if you eat peas, or people who eat crabs end up living longer than everyone else.

It is targeted at providing benefits that look too beautiful to ignore. The victim is willing to do it already.

There is a propaganda technique called the education method. This is used to cover lapses in case you disagree with what's been taught. The aim is to still lure the victim into believing "it is majorly for his benefit. It is portrayed as having something to lose if you would not do it, so it comes with the label, do it because it is the right thing any sane person will do).

Brainwashing is a drastic way to cause sincere damage to a person's way of thinking and living without the person's approval or knowledge. It gives you the impression that it's your idea all along, so you won't notice you are being broken.

However, brainwashing is such an interfering form of effect. It requires the victim to be separated from everyone or thing and be solely dependent on the person causing the damage, that is, the brainwasher. These are part of the reasons why brainwashing escapades are more rampant at prison yards, communist society, cults, and the likes because it's a form of mind imprisonment.

In brainwashing, the brainwasher must assume total control over the victim. The victim will have to depend upon the brainwasher for many things he should typically do for himself, things like sleeping, eating, using the bathroom,   and other essential things. Brainwashing processes include shutting out the victim's conviction, attitude, behavior, opinion, and replacing them with new ones.

Psychologists around the world do have different opinions about brainwashing. They do not all agree on the same thing. Some agree that it is indeed possible in the right settings, while some believe it is possible. Some even go as far as saying it is not as dangerous as the media portrays it. In contrast, others admit that it involves physical threat to persuade the victim to adhere to what is required to achieve their desired results.

Psychologists also believe the victim's initial identity is merely hiding and would surface if left without torture for some time. Some agreed to the fact that the identity will be lost depending on the person causing the damage.

Sometimes in 1950, a psychologist named Robert Jay Lifton watched some prisoners of the Korean war and the Chinese war camp only to deduce that they had gone through. A diversified phase began with the captives' self-worth and ended with the captives' conviction.

Robert seeing this, quickly identified the process involved.

- Attack on personality
- Burden /guilt
- Self-denial
- Shattering juncture
- Mercy
- The compulsion to admit guilt
- Funneling of grief
- Disclosing of grief
- Improvement and unity
- The last admission and regeneration

All the processes above happen in a place of solitude where only the target is confined. Here, there will be no social life amenities. A lot of depriving is done to change the mind of the target. Things like malnutrition and sleep deprivation are mind fogging techniques. It's part of the process required to brainwash an individual.

Of course, all this happens with bodily harm threats to retard the targets thinking and independence.

We can compress Lifton's process into three-part which includes

1. Breaking down the personality

2. The introduction of a new concept
3. Rebuilding the self

BREAKING DOWN THE PERSONALITY

Assault on Personality

The first step in this procedure is making the victim believe he does not have a clue about himself. The assault often comes in accusing sentences. They make what you think you are worthless, such that you start doubting your existence. The procedure will leave you confused and disoriented. Everything you think you know will be thrown into the garbage. This is called this deletion process.

Remarks like: "you are not what you think you are," "you are not a man." These will continue for days, weeks, months, along with as it takes you to believe what you have been served and leave yours in the trash. Thus, the ego is completely crushed.

Guilt

Before he finishes processing the personality demolition, another attack is placed on the victim. This attack is often aimed at generating guilt in the victim. It is fashioned to condemn everything he does, from talking like an imbecile and nailing it all on his former beliefs to the demon in him that gives him his initial thoughts. It often comes in a direct accusation like, "you are evil." This way, the victim is scrutinized of any sin, told of his sins, and makes him wonder if he can find redemption.

Self Betrayal

Admit that you are evil! This and more are the many words thrown into the victim's shaking mind waiting to be shattered; this way, the victim is forced to reduce all that he has, known, seen, or entitled to. All this, in turn, is to increase the pressure on the already shaky mind.

Breaking Point

Loss of identity leads to questions like "who am I?" "what am I?" Questions. It's like amnesia because the victim is caught up in confusion, guilt, shame, betrayal, and so on. He or she already loses their grip on self-esteem—issues like a nervous breakdown, ill mind, and many more.

However, the nervous breakdown has its symptoms like uncontrolled sobbing, shying away from humans, wanting to be in the dark, depression, and disorientation, to mention a few. The victim will by this time lose contact with reality, feel lost and alone. Once the victim has been broken, they are empty inside, so any assistance is highly welcome, and the programming starts.

THE POSSIBILITY OF SALVATION

Mercy

The victim here is an empty, cracked mind who already started away from reality. Here an offer of help will look like someone holding out a hand to help you out of a pit, so the victim succumbs quickly at the mention of help. At this point, the victim is offered what he or she is most deprived of. At this phase, easy access is gained into the mind.

The Compulsion To Confession

Here the victim is faced with the reality of both guilt and pain, of the bombardment of personality demolition. So the only presented way out is to confess to him supposedly things he had done. The relief of mercy shown will lure the victim into returning the act of kindness from the harasser.

Funneling of Guilt

The victim knows he is wrong at this junction, but he would not know for what reason. So the harasser will be there to fill in the gap, making him believe all along, he caused his shame and pain through his conviction and opinion. They often present the victim that his formal conviction has brought such calamity and that the new belief will solve his problem.

Releasing Of Guilt

In this process, the victim is made to understand. He is not even a problem. After all, it is mainly his conviction to be free from this burden of guilt, wrong name, and all other things that have been done to him. He will have to let go of his guilt, opinion, people he knows and loves, everything dear to him. It is just like equipping him with a weapon to fight his existence.

The confused mind will now relax at the thought of an escape plan and laden himself with the idea of getting out. Can you imagine the determination and joy at a ray of hope? Knowing that the way out of his misery is gazing him right in the eye, he will release his old belief and organization willing and wait upon the brainwasher to offer him salvation with this knowledge.

REBUILDING THE SELF

Progress And Harmony

The strategy is to throw an open question your way, making you think it's all in your hands to decide whether to do good or remain evil. It's like telling the victim, "you still have the opportunity to be a good person," "all you need is to choose which way to go." After putting a latch to his neck while mounting pressure on it all along.

What level of mockery is that you may think, making him believe his redemption lies in his own hands. When typically, he doesn't even have a clue what's happened to him. This stage involves the brainwasher placing himself as the person to provide that "good," which is the new belief system.

Final Confession And Rebirth

This is a moment of absorption, graduation, initiation, and every other word that looks like it. Here the victim accepts and pledges allegiance to the new and only redemption for him, that seems right, although a make-belief. There are rites to be performed to welcome the recruit into their midst. The new vegetable(victim) starts seeing himself showered, undeserved love. He will feel indebted to the brainwashers for giving him something more than gold. He will see them as Messiah. These whole processes are described as rebirth by some victims.

The scenario described above has not been tested at any modern laboratory. It will be severe for the victim and would be an immoral, scientific examination. Robert Jay Lifton designed this description from his studying the Korean way of brainwashing the Prisoners of War and other instances gathered worldwide.

Lifton and other psychologists around the world noticed the differences in the brainwashing procedure. They concluded from the observations so far that with the rate at which the victims are often bombarded under the same conditions, some victims still escape being broken. At the same time, some would not take long to be broken.

It is somehow concluded that initial personality traits could contribute to the outcome of the whole brainwashing procedure. They observed that people with a weak mind resolution, low self-esteem, traumatic conditions, self-doubt, lack of self-confidence are effortlessly drawn into the brainwashing damage. While people with a strong mind, confidence, people who believe in themselves are more difficult to break no matter the medium.

Having gained this knowledge about the POWs and what they suffered, courses have been put in place to counter brainwashing if any military officer is held captive. Research believes that understanding of the process will make breaking impossible. So there are various courses available at the Military's disposal to tap into the knowledge and resistance of brainwashing such that they will still retain their identity no matter the technique used to break them.

THE MODERN-DAY WEAPON

The idea of brainwashing has been in place for a longer time than imagined, but the U.S caught a glimpse of it in 1950 during the Korean war. Political prisoners are often deceived by the word "re-education" by the Russian Communists. Brainwashing starts as a greedy way of canceling someone's belief regardless of what it means to them and feeding them with your view of the world instead.

This exactly was the events that unfold at the Russian prisoners camp in the name of "thought reform." A Chinese writer, Chairman Mao Tse-tung's writing in "The Little Red Book" published the world's whole idea to see.

Mao Tse-tung used the phrase "ssu-Hsiang- to -cheng," which means thought struggle) to explain the brainwashing method. Mao-tung had later become the head of the Chinese communist in 1929. A lot of political prisoners suffered brainwashing at the hands of the communist right there in China.

Edward Hunter had been the first person to use the phrase "brainwashing" in 1951. He had used the term to describe how the

American POWs were treated during the Korean War. Edward made public the theory that when most Americans are already frightened when they have zero ideas about what's going on, they fear being converted without their approval. Edward's approach came in handy.

The U.S had plunged neck-deep into researching the type of drugs and the effects used in the mind-altering process. The U.S was afraid she was losing her ground in the latest weaponry race. She put in place a scheme called MKULTRAL from the CIA department. The technique employed by the CIA department didn't produce a favorable result. Instead, it was more harmful than usual because it is a brainwashing procedure with a friendly approach.

Patty Hearst's story, the heiress to the Hearst publishing fortune, is a famous story about how brainwashing works and how far it goes.

She was brainwashed after being kidnapped in the 1970s. She mentioned being locked in a dark room for some days, left hungry, brutalized while her mind is being repeatedly assaulted. Hearst noted being made to renounce her faith and family. She even renamed her family "Pig Hearst." She was later prosecuted for robbery in 1979 when she blamed it all on being brainwashed even though she was caught on security tape. Hearst later went to jail for seven years, but her sentence was commuted after two years by President Carter.

"Insanity by brainwashing" is Lee Boyd Malvo's famous story 30 years after Patty Hearst'. Lee Boyd Malvo was also prosecuted in

2002 for taking part in a sniper attack within and without Washington, D.C. Malvo, who was 17years at the time, had partnered with a 42-year-old John Allen Muhammad. They had allegedly killed ten people and subject 3 to physical damage, all in a killing rampage. His defense claimed that the 42-year-old John had brainwashed Malvo, who would not have been found in John's company talkless of killing him without being brainwashed. Contrary to the defense plea, Malvo ends up bagging life imprisonment without parole while John was sentenced to death.

The jury tends to see brainwashing as a modern mask of shying away from taking responsibility for the crime committed. Hence, the sentencing, no matter the brainwashed claims.

Looking into the future with Hollywood theory, the future of brainwashing is bound to be savage and frightful than now and before. It is believed that higher gadgets will be in place much more toxic than the existing ones. Likewise, it is expected that as the world evolves with safe technology, unsafe technology also exists, which will further endanger the lives of future victims.

BRAINWASHING TECHNIQUES

Consider each of the cases you see in the media daily. Advertisers are among the violators, along with major cable news networks such as Fox News, CNN, and others. When the press force-led opinions and ideas like which group is evil and which one is better and begin to see reason with them, you are being brainwashed.

The same applies to advertisements. An advertiser continues to tell you repeatedly that a particular product is better than the other. In a short while, you will find yourself not just buying the product but also telling other people about it.

Just consider it. Did you do a study that came to these decisions? Did you try the product labeled as bad? It's unlikely, but you probably already agree with advertisers' opinion. That's brainwashing at its best.

There are very few fundamental tactics to successfully brainwashing individuals. The amusing part is that you will realize many of these approaches being used on you in your daily life.

Writer Edward Hunter contrived the word "brainwashing" to portray the re-training strategies that the Chinese utilized on American officers caught during the war.

The term has since become related to cult groups, which frequently use a blend of psychological procedures to leave their members willing. The psychologist Margaret Singer believed that at any particular time, Roughly 2.5 million individuals in only the United States are members of known cults who use brainwashing strategies on members.

On the other hand, the notion of brainwashing has always been contentious. Hunter has been related to the intelligence community. It's been indicated that the CIA promoted the expression as a simple means to explain the rapid development of Communism at the moment.

The founders Robert Lifton and Edgar Schein reasoned that the American prisoners of wars who left anti-American statements largely did to avoid physical punishment. That the POWs' brainwashing was not successful. It's essential to bear in mind that there's some disagreement about what precisely constitutes brainwashing and how successful it could be.

Chanting and Singing Slogans

Chanting slogans is a significant characteristic of several religions, notably Buddhism and Hinduism. Virtually every church or Islamic body has some hymn-singing worship. As every member of their team chants or sings the same words, their voices blend into a single chorus, a powerful sense of oneness and group identity shapes. This, together with known effects of singing such as reduced pulse and comfort, may throw the team worship experience favorably.

However, in cults, the persistent repetition of brief intonations was made to develop into mind-numbing, eliminating rational thinking and causing a trance state. Heightened suggestibility is a characteristic of this kind of condition. Failure to keep the trance can be accompanied by cult-inflicted punishment, making sure ultra-conformist behavior is always enforced.

Psychologists have analyzed how exposure to repeated and protracted hypnotic inductions can alter the convert's capacity to make decisions and assess new information. Additionally, constant teachings, singing, and chanting are used by most cults to change the consciousness of many followers. In this manner, hypnosis through chanting is a tool used by cult leaders to hamper critical thinking skills instead of coordinating purposes.

In cases like this, the followers or members of the cult or religious body get brainwashed unconsciously through a gradual and seemingly harmless process.

The further you hear something, the more suggestive it becomes. If you were told day in and day out that you walk in a certain way, even though you know you do not, you will start to believe the repeated comments after some time.

So the same is true for different things, also. If you're told your sneakers smell every day, but you don't think it does. At some point, you will because you will feel you are making other people inconvenient, and we generally do not like that type of feeling.

Isolation

In 1977, Jim Jones and approximately 1,000 members of the People's Temple spiritual group moved to Guyana's isolated community. The distance between the settlement in the jungle and the US Embassy was more than 400 km (250 mi) in the Guyanese capital Georgetown. Such confinement helped the cultists dispose of consideration on the outside world's interruptions, giving Jones the liberty to impart his alarming system.

People who contradicted Jones could be set to tranquilize actuated trance states or have pythons folded around their necks. Rebellious children were reduced into dark wells at nighttime.

The cult's geographic isolation was consequently paralleled with a psychological one. A long way from the interruptions of loved ones in the US, with boorish discipline awaiting them when they refuse to adjust, the individuals from the People's Temple had minimal other options than to mutely follow Jones' harmful philosophies. In any event, when they had been internally uncomfortable with what had been happening.

In its whole command over its people and implemented seclusion, the People's Temple Agricultural Project bears correlation with untouchable countries like North Korea or even pre-1991 Albania.

We have seen similar brainwashing techniques applied by terrorist groups. They isolate their members and instill their teaching into them before releasing them to go and carry out dastardly acts that lead to the loss of lives and property.

Isolation is also applied by spouses who brainwashed their partners. Partners use these tactics to cut the other away from their family and friends. In some cases, they relocate physically to places where the other partner has no options but ultimately relies on them.

Dependency and Fear

A classic example of brainwashing through abduction and fear is the 1974 kidnap of heiress Patty Hearst by the Symbionese Liberation Army. The terrorist group responsible for multiple bank robberies and murders camped close to where Hearst lived. Hearst was kidnapped and quickly changed from a young socialite into a bank robber and seemingly dedicated member of a terrorist association.

While in captivity, Hearst was told repeatedly that she would be killed at any moment. This is in addition to being locked away in a cupboard and enduring constant physical and emotional abuses.

The Symbionese Liberation Army had complete control over Hearst.

This reliance on her captors resulted in the renowned effect of capture-bonding or Stockholm Syndrome. After some months, she emerged as an ideologically dedicated member of their organization, even engaging in a San Francisco bank robbery.

After her arrest, her defense of being brainwashed failed as the trial judge agreed with the prosecution that she completely and willingly complied with the terrorist group. Patty Hearst was sentenced to serve seven years behind bars.

President Carter later commuted her sentence to 2 years due to the "degrading experience" she suffered at her captors' hands. Hearst might seem to have been more susceptible than others; her story shows how debilitating experiences can alter who we are and what we think.

Making people believe the world could detonate under them at any second is an extraordinary method to control somebody. If you offer somebody your wing, they will have a sense of security, causing a manipulator's plans to seem like the right ones.

Dependency and feat are standard control techniques with human traffickers and slavery. The manipulator brainwashes the victim into believing they will be arrested and thrown to jail or even die if they do not abide by specific rules. The victims, in turn, obey the manipulator as though their lives depended on it. In some cases, it does.

Emotions permit manipulation, particularly when feelings are related to dread and misery. Causing an individual to feel awful when they don't conform to wishes or making somebody terrified not to do the "right" thing can force them into doing what is wanted by the brainwasher.

Activity Teaching and Physical Exercise

How can a teacher promote decent behavior and compliance with rules in their pupils? The response often entails integrating some physical activity or game in their teaching. When kids are absorbed in jumping up and down and running around and exhausted, they are less inclined to assert or create trouble.

Recognizing this occurrence, many cults have aimed to inhabit members using an infinite set of exhausting activities as a way of control. For instance, some cults such as Dahn Yoga are, on the surface, only physical exercise programs.

In Russia, mass sporting events such as aerobics in stadiums have been a familiar characteristic of the Soviet system. They are connected by historians using the repressive state apparatus.

What distinguishes action pedagogy from sports is that a cult or regime will benefit from the increased mood and team identity undergone after physical activity to present ideological beliefs that may otherwise be met with disbelief.

Exhaustion by practice is still another way that people's defenses could be worn out as a way of inviting them to take questionable ideas.

Finger Pointing and Criticism

Throughout the Korean War, American soldiers captured by the Chinese were exposed to rebuke and self-criticism sessions. They needed to denounce fellow Americans, say their flaws, and express their insecurities regarding capitalism and the United States. In the beginning, the Prisoners of War believed the sessions were child's play. As time passed, the continuing criticism process began to manifest real doubts regarding their patriotism and the war's legitimacy.

The prisoners' growing anxiety impacts this "Rule of Commitment." It states that we try to make our ideas consistent with our public comments because we don't want to become unpredictable or dishonest.

Despite some limited successes, the Korean War brainwashing methods were not especially effective. Just 23 Prisoners of War refused repatriation at the end of the war. The Chinese had primarily abandoned the reeducation sessions before the war ended. However, they continued to use similar practices with their citizens.

Rule of Commitment

Have you tried changing your mind in the middle of a transaction because you find out what spikes your interest at first isn't worth it much later, and you had a second thought? Have you ever been boxed in, and changing your mind becomes impossible such that you had no choice but to continue with the investment because of a sense of obligation or attachment?

If yes! How did you maneuver, did you pull back, or you felt an invisible string pulling you to go ahead with the purchase no matter what?

The above description is what is known as the "Rule of Commitment."

This term refers to the general norm used by salespeople or marketers when they want to close a business deal. They employ this strategy by coaxing their prospects, making them know what they needed them to see. In this pattern, we are laden with the responsibility to follow through with the deal because we think we have agreed.

You may ask why? We like to assume that we have integrity, and it should reflect on our attitude and our conviction. Hence, when we make some announcement, we sometimes feel the need to stand solidly by our words.

Most times, this norm of commitment can work to our charm. Imagine telling our family and friends about our decisions to get on a better diet, a particular body shape, or something we think it's important at the time. You think it will be better to get it done as our family members or friends will be a better reminder than an electrical device. Their dedication to us can surpass that of a mere clock. This exactly can land us in situations beyond our control, as it may not be relevant to us again, but the fact that they are already aware, we might be pestered into doing it.

Norm Of Commitment In Action

Marketers have found a way to use this norm to their advantage. A lot of coaxing strategy that goes in tune with this commitment rule triggers a positive response from prospective buyers. There is a popular strategy called the "low-ball" strategy. In this method, the salesperson makes the goods' cost appear lesser than raising it after committing to the transaction. This, in turn, triggers obligated feelings in the consumer to go along with the initial plan.

Another frequently used sales technique is the foot-in-the-door strategy. According to this strategy, the salesperson starts by making little demands; when you consent to this, they make greater demands. At the same time, luring you to feel responsible for the whole plan while making it look like your idea after all.

Making Commitment On Your Behalf

The strength of commitment often lures one to hold on to the plans that do not correlate with our wants or needs, like committing to buy an overpriced item. However, this trend is not a bad influence on our habits. One might end up realizing the rule of commitment can be used to influence positive behavioral changes.

Have you ever tried giving up an addictive behavior like drinking, smoking, hard drugs, or finishing a particular project which requires commitment? Do you know that telling it to your family and friends may be the only way to achieve a successful result on the decision? Family and friends awareness tends to be a strong influence and reminder than any gadget we might want to employ to our aim. This also is an example of the rule of commitment.

Sleep Deprivation

Sleep deprivation leads to sensory overload, disorientation, and stimulation, which alters our capacity to make the right decisions. Amway was accused of depriving its vendors of sleep through weekend-long functions. These comprise nonstop lectures running into the wee hours of the afternoon, with only brief interludes during which groups play loud music full of flashing lights.

Some cult techniques occasionally use sleep deprivation and teaching members to follow special diets containing low protein levels and other vital nutrients. Asa result, the cult members will probably always feel tired, making them helpless to withstand cult ideology orders.

During the 20th commemoration of the Aum Shinrikyo Sarin nerve gas assault, the Japan Times interviewed a former cult member. He described his ordeal and how they were "eating a single meal each day and resting for a couple of hours every night." All these, while trying to get the Cult chief elected into parliament.

Love Bombing

Love Bombing is a practice common with cults. They use this practice to lure people into the group, lavish them with affection or attention to influence or manipulate them.

Cults and groups tend to re-establish the concept that the outside world, distinct from their gathering, is hostile and in terrible blunder. To create a friendly atmosphere different from the world's hostility, they often use "love bombing," all for the positive response. Love bombing includes lavishing fresh or proposed followers with an elaborated set of attention and care.

The idea originated from The Unification Church or The Children of God. However, this conclusion has since been utilized by a broad scope of associations.

[129]

It is a routine work of psychology that we feel attached to retaliate others' good deeds and magnificence. So, the false love, persuasion, and mutual trust portrayed by existing cult members towards the recruit are fashioned to make a progressive understanding of duty, liability, and low self-esteem. All these are effective because freshers want a feel of belonging and approval.

People are initiated into a cult through a process of unfreezing and refreezing, which we might call "evaporating and ensnaring." During the refreezing, a prospective cult member deletes the world's initial design while embracing the cults' supposed perfect plan.

Mystical Manipulation

Many cults rely on mystical manipulations to gain the genuine interest of their follower's minds. Mysterious manipulations, however, mean gaining absolute power of situations, circumstance, or news by a sect leader to portray the belief that they possess the authority of remarkable wisdom and divine benefit mysterious power.

In other words, professed religious leaders present themselves as God's inerrant messenger whose train of thoughts must always be sincere and confirm while supporting this through strange tactics. Most times, these supposed leaders are the mastermind behind the manipulative happenings; they claim to be divine.

There was once an event that happened between David Koresh and George Roden. George Roden had once challenged David Koresh in the quest to be a leader for the Davidian Branch. George had suggested exhuming a corpse and had done just that to perform his necromancy skills. He had hoped to bring the dead to life and also challenged Koresh to do the same.

Instead, Koresh had gone to report him to the governments who requested evidence of George's act. In entering the place where George's experiment is taking place, a gunfight erupts between Koresh, the governments, and George's aides.

Koresh's initial name is Vernon Howell, but he changed it to tell the world that the biblical King David is his ancestor. His last name Koresh was farther after a Persian ruler named Cyrus the Great. He delivered the news from the Babylonian captivity.

Koresh created a messianic persona and again advised his fans to categorize the unusual happenings to heavenly intervention instead of confessing he devised them.

During the refreezing phase, the sect seals this new identity. However, members who embrace this other rule of living get applauded and hugged once they cross the lines by wanting to know more, they are ignored.

Today, our world is filled with brainwashed people who unconsciously are members of a cult but cannot see it now because they have been brainwashed.

Barratrous Abuse

Representatives of the cult who denounce their faith become unbreakable by any external means. The sect does not take any charge for granted, either hate speech or any form of charge used by anyone regardless of the traditional loyalties.

The cults do not care if they lose or win since they know the departed-member will never be free from their freezing. The pasts-representatives are left broken with no power to mount an effective lawsuit.

The existence of legal action makes it impossible for a journalist to dabble into Celtic issues. Cult Like cases once led an investigator named Rick Ross to get gleans from the manuals of NXIVM in 2003.

Rick Ross posted the gleans online, and investigators were hired against him to look through his files, and they filed a lawsuit against him. NXIVM, however, has again suffered several prosecutions from their employees, though they remain intact.

We also know Scientology for a ridiculous lawsuit to discourage antagonists. Someone in the person, Lon. Ron Hubbard once wrote that they find no Scientology attacker with a plain past. They all have criminal records. It is concluded that most lawsuits are targeted at harassment rather than winning.

Abuse is usually one of the brainwashing tactics that most devotees fight their victims into staying quiet.

Thought-Terminating Cliches

One other important notion is that undemocratic regimes rely upon thought-terminating clichés to conform to their followers' conformity. Numerous extensive and confounded human issues are packed into brief, exceptionally reductive, authoritative-sounding expressions through these adages.

For instance, the all-encompassing sources of Communist regimes such as China and the Soviet Union, in which speech became subjective, highly categorical, relentlessly stressing, and finally, the vocabulary of non-thought.

The Soviet Union's love of this type of jargon before inspired George Orwell's book 1984, the oppressive government lays out a language named Newspeak to curb the capacity to think except in relation defined by the country. Modern non-state groups such as the Church of Scientology could be considered to have developed a pair of phrases roughly equal to the Soviet slang.

The most well-known illustration of thought-terminating clichés likely comes in the trial of Nazi Adolf Eichmann. The SS leader often spoke in stock phrases and clichés. Eichmann repeated he wished to make peace with his former foes. The term was meaningless since he did not know the magnitude of his crimes in any way.

He could only conceive of these in the speech of National Socialism. The entire eighty million German populace was impeded against the real world and factuality correctly similarly, a similar self-duplicity, untruths, and idiocy.

We have all experienced and expressed thought-terminating cliches in our daily lives. These cliches prevent us from thinking outside the box or objectively. It makes us accept what has been thrown at us as the "end of the matter."

Like when some lose their job, we say, " well, stuff happened," "it's the depression," and all sorts. These are cliches preventing us from probing further and suggesting there should be no further discussion on the topic.

Another example is when a child comes home from school with bruises. Rather than the parent probing for details, they may choose to go with the cliche, "Kids will always be kids," or "boys will be boys." This settles the matter for the parent. They don't know if it results from the child being bullied or other underlying deeper issues.

Cliches affect how people think and accept things around them. Have you heard something like, "it's the Will of God" when someone dies? That explains everything. In some cases, there will be no further investigations into what led to the death of the individual involved.

A SHORT MESSAGE FROM HAPPINESS FACTORY

Hey, are you enjoying the book? We'd love to hear your thoughts!

Many readers do not know how hard reviews are to come by and how much they help an author.

We would be incredibly thankful if you could take just 60 seconds to write a brief review on Amazon, even if it's just a few sentences!

>> Click here to leave a quick review

Thank you for taking the time to share your thoughts!

Your review will genuinely make a difference for me and help me gain exposure to our work.

EMOTIONAL INTELLIGENCE - EQ/EI

Many of us are conscious of our IQ (Intelligence Quotient) and, in some instances, the IQ of other people. When we come across people who are successful academically or in different life facets, we are quick to associate it with their IQ level.

The IQ is designed to measure the intellectual intellect, and it provides a score by a collection of tests. Greater IQs suggest better problem-solving skills or the capacity to learn and comprehend. People with higher IQs are bound to perform remarkably better without applying similar mental exertion measures as individuals with lower IQ scores.

Thus, a logical premise is that individuals with higher IQs are successful in the office and life. This premise was proven wrong. There's much more to success than just being smart.

Emotional Intelligence (EI or EQ - Emotional Quotient) is an advanced thought and was just completely evolved during the 1990s, by Daniel Goleman.

Emotional Intelligence is your measure of someone's capacity to comprehend and handle their emotions as well as other people's feelings, both independently and in teams.

Emotional intelligence talks about the capability to comprehend, control, and assess emotions. Some studies indicate that emotional intelligence can be learned and fortified, but some claim it is an inborn trait.

The capacity to communicate and control feelings is vital, but so is your ability to comprehend, interpret, and react to others' feelings. Envision a universe where you could not figure out when a friend is unhappy or if a co-worker was livid. Emotional intelligence is not just about your emotions alone but that of the other people in your environment.

Psychologists refer to the ability to feel and understand how others feel as emotional intelligence. Several experts suggest it could be a higher priority than IQ regarding by and large achievement throughout everyday life.

We use emotional intelligence when we grapple with our colleagues and have in-depth discussions about our relationships with our spouses. It also comes to play when we need to handle an uncontrollable or agitated child. It allows us to interface with others, get ourselves, and live a more credible, stable, and happy way of life.

Even though many intelligence types are frequently linked, there are many quite essential differences between them.

IMPORTANCE OF EMOTIONAL INTELLIGENCE

Emotional intelligence is the ability to comprehend and manage your own emotions.

It's become a small popular word in human resources departments throughout the planet, but scientists say that it's time emotional intelligence be taken seriously. Embracing human emotion subtlety at work may have practical advantages, including better cooperation among employees and a happier office. We're human beings daily, not only when we depart the workplace.

It is a scientific reality that emotions precede thought. When emotions run high, they alter how our brains operate, decreasing our cognitive skills, decision-making abilities, and even social skills. Recognizing and handling our emotions and others helps us become more effective in our private and professional lives.

On an individual level, emotional intelligence helps us.

- Have embarrassing conversations without damaging each other's feelings
- Handle our feelings if stressed or feeling helpless
- Boost relationships with all the people we care for

At the office, emotional intelligence helps us.

- In conflict resolutions
- Train and inspire others
- Produce a culture of cooperation
- Construct psychological security within groups

Figuring out your emotions is essential to understanding what will lead one to flourish and be more effective. That is because, as individuals, we tend to be extremely social and emotional beings.

EQ can help you when interfacing with others, upgrade your work execution, better your relational abilities, become more robust, and significantly more. It turns out that having a top EQ level can cause you to be successful in pretty much every single part of your daily life.

ADDRESSING OUR FEELINGS

The unfortunate tendency that has swept western society would be comprehending and handling human feelings entirely. This tendency has spilled into different regions of life, including the workplace. While emotions tend to be left at the door once you start work, this has catastrophic consequences on organizations and workers. After all, we are emotional individuals.

However, companies are shifting and are starting to give extensive and personal work arrangements and new services. For instance, some health plans include mental health policy to ensure individuals at work are cared for.

Including hiring psychologists for human resources groups: getting to know that your workforce is as best as possible and supplying valuable training that directly leads to employee/employer relationships.

As we all know, it is not the most brilliant folks who are the most effective or very fulfilled in life. You probably know academically brilliant, socially inept, and unsuccessful people in their career or their relationships.

The intellectual skill or your intelligence quotient (IQ) is not sufficient on its own to attain success in your life. Your IQ will help you get into school, but your EQ will help you handle the tension and emotions when confronting your last exams. Levels of emotional intelligence and IQ exist in pairs and are best when they work off each other.

ACADEMICALLY/WORK ACHIEVEMENT

High emotional intelligence can help you sail through the office's social issues, lead and inspire other people, and excel in your career. In reality, when it comes to measuring key job applicants, many companies today rate emotional intelligence as important as technical skill and use EQ testing before hiring. Your IQ will land you the position. However, it's your EQ that will keep you at work and help you ascend the professional stepping stool.

Daily we create emotionally influenced choices. We believe the first strategy is way better than the other. We occasionally make decisions based on our feelings or gut feelings. As soon as we know the source and origin of these feelings, mainly if working in a group, we are more connected and likely trust each other's decision.

Due to globalization, emotional intelligence is even more critical now when groups are cross-cultural and international, raising feelings' complexity and how they are expressed. Basically, emotional intelligence at work boils down to understanding, communicating, and handling perfect connections, and solving problems under pressure.

Companies who intentionally recruit and see the growth and improvement of their workforce's emotional intelligence will function to maximum efficacy. Emotional intelligence only raises

[140]

the business's success, regardless of how that achievement is measured. The main point is that it's vital for business excellence.

EQ can work amazing things for your company because applying it will cause you to realize how relationships and people operate.

Emotionally intelligent colleagues will consistently dominate in authority, cooperation, organization, and vision. They will know their associations with different representatives, groups, directors, customers, contenders, media associations.

A group of emotionally smart individuals employs staff members who are motivated, successful, efficient, powerful, honored, and likable, and their aims will be aligned with the company's plan.

This is only because EQ applies to each human interaction in the company; using a top average EQ staff can improve customer support, brainstorming sessions, business presentations, and myriad other tasks.

Emotional intelligence at work can help you evaluate people better, understand how relationships grow, understand our beliefs, create our adventures, and learn how to stop power struggles, negative judgment, immunity, etc., to raise success and vision.

PHYSICAL WELL-BEING.

If you cannot handle your emotions, you're most likely not managing your anxiety. This may result in serious health issues. Uncontrolled stress increases blood pressure, suppresses the immune system, raises the chance of heart attacks and strokes, leads to infertility, and accelerates the aging procedure. The very first step to enhancing emotional intelligence would be to understand how to control anxiety.

SOCIAL INTELLECT

Being in accordance with your emotions fills in as a social capacity, associating you to others and your overall environmental factors. Social knowledge allows you to identify a companion from an enemy, evaluate someone else's advantage as a part of your character, lessen pressure, balance your sensory system through social interactions, and feel glad and cherished.

PSYCHOLOGICAL WELLNESS.

Unchecked emotions and anxiety can also affect your mental health, making you vulnerable to stress and depression. If you can understand, get familiar with, or handle your emotions, you'll also fight to retain strong relationships. This, then, can leave you feeling isolated and lonely and further aggravate any emotional health issues.

YOUR RELATIONSHIPS

Having a better understanding of your emotions helps you know how to maneuver them. You are better equipped to express yourself and learn how others feel. This allows you to communicate more efficiently and forge stronger connections, both in the office and in your private life.

Communication contributes directly to why it is imperative to create emotional intelligence, building and keeping up solid relationships.

It's easy to see how using a high EQ may result in better relationships.

Individuals with high emotional intelligence can:

- Read other people's feelings and suitably and efficiently respond to them.
- They know and control their emotions, so do not bottle things up or allow negative emotions to burst from them.
- Understand that their thoughts produce their feelings, and regulating these ideas makes it possible for them to control their emotions.
- Align their actions to other people's emotional reactions. They understand the impacts their actions will have on other people and how others may feel and react.

It is no wonder that highly emotionally intelligent individuals have more secure, pleasing, and high-quality relationships than people with low emotional intelligence.

Emotionally intelligent people notice how others feel, respond appropriately to other people, regulate their own emotions, and observe their behavior to guarantee they do not unnecessarily offend or upset others. All these are the components of a healthy, respectful relationship, while that connection is between fans, friends, family, or coworkers.

SELF-MANAGEMENT

Self-management is of the vital skills required in life. Not only does it help us live happier, healthier lives, but it also helps us throughout the day, tough days.

Self-management is the initial measure. We have to learn how to handle ourselves before managing healthy, proper relationships with others. Learning self-management makes you control your emotions and inspire yourself in most scenarios.

RELATIONSHIP MANAGEMENT

Enhancing your relationship management abilities permits you to develop healthy relationships and communicate effectively in most circumstances, such as being open with other people, getting your point across, persuading others, and being truthful without alienating or offending others.

Developing your emotional intelligence can assist you with this vital ability, along with other skills. For instance, emotional intelligence can help you in the office, if you're an employee, a supervisor, or the company owner.

DECISION MAKING

EQ will enhance decision-making skills. Those people who have a great understanding of themselves and other people around them are far more inclined to weigh all of the choices, maintain an open mind, and eliminate all immaterial emotions in the decision-making procedure.

It is worth noting that individuals with high EQs do not eliminate all of the emotions in their conclusion, just those which may interfere, like stress. This helps them remain more goal-oriented while also letting them rely on their feelings to a great extent.

EQ FOR COMMUNICATION

EQ is closely linked with communication abilities; individuals with high emotional intelligence are inclined to be adept in their communication skills.

People With High Emotional Intelligence:

- Consider other people's feelings.
- Respect their feelings
- Practice compassion for others and relate to them in a conversation
- Run-on confidence, meaning that they build trust through nonverbal and verbal cues and convey frankly;
- Recognize, identify, and clear up any misunderstandings

The list shows how EQ impacts communication: A top EQ contributes to proficiency in discussions. The ability to communicate is needed for a healthy personal life and a healthier professional life.

For Building Resilience

Emotional intelligence is unquestionably a valuable instrument to use in the face of hardship. It can improve not just leadership skills and teamwork efficacy but also personal elasticity.

Focusing on the influence of emotional intelligence on resilience, one can deal with stressful circumstances. The study indicates that individuals who exhibit greater emotional intelligence levels are not as likely to succumb to stressors' adverse effects.

[145]

In a leadership function situation, an individual might expect greater obligation to coincide with elevated possible stressors, emphasizing the value of high emotional intelligence for people in leadership or management positions.

A study into the connection between emotional intelligence and the stress procedure found that participants who exhibited higher emotional intelligence were not as likely to be more negatively affected by stress.

Participants performed an ability-based evaluation of emotional intelligence earlier evaluation of the subjectively perceived threat level posed by two stressors. Then they self-reported their psychological reaction to stated stressors and were subjected to physiological stress-response assessment to evaluate their response.

The findings indicated that emotional intelligence aspects were associated with reduced hazard appraisals, smaller declines in positive influence, less negative impact, and challenge physiological reactions to stress. This analysis offers predictive validity, which emotional intelligence alleviates stress resilience.

An additional study suggested a connection between greater emotional intelligence, endurance, and the propensity for depressive behaviors in analyzing medical professionals—a job with a comparatively high "burnout" rate. Studies reveal a positive correlation between emotional intelligence and endurance and a negative correlation between persistence, mindfulness, and self-compassion, and all the burnout level.

In brief, people who have greater emotional intelligence levels also shown more outstanding durability and were less inclined to burnout' or succumb to depression.

These results build on the past study, which discovered EQ scores were positively associated with emotional well-being while negatively correlated with burnout and depression. Given EQ's energetic nature, the analysis emphasized the possible capability to reduce the susceptibility to depression through interventions to improve emotional intelligence.

Interestingly, EQ is closely connected with individual improvement and functionality, with evidence indicating a substantial connection between motivation and durability to achieve.

What's more, it's implied that resilience plays a mediational role between emotional intelligence and self-motivated success. To put it differently, emotional intelligence is a necessity for resilience, and resilience may result in greater motivation. Resilience comes with an inherent perseverance element that inspires endurance in the face of challenges.

COMPONENTS OF EMOTIONAL INTELLIGENCE

The abilities which make up emotional intelligence can be learned at any given moment. However, it is essential not to forget there is a difference between studying EQ and applying that understanding to your life. Simply because you are aware you ought to do something does not mean that you will, significantly once you become overwhelmed with anxiety, which may overturn your purpose.

To permanently change behavior in a way that stands up under stress, you have to understand how to conquer anxiety in the present time and in your relationships to stay emotionally conscious.

The critical skills for constructing your EQ and enhancing your ability to handle feelings and join with other people comprise five distinct elements.

SELF REGULATION

This facet of EI requires the proper expression of emotion. Self-regulation includes being elastic, coping with change, and handling conflict. Additionally, it describes diffusing difficult or nervous conditions, being conscious of how one's actions affect other people and taking possession of those activities.

If you must put your EQ to work, then you ought to have the ability to use your emotions to make constructive decisions regarding your behavior. When you become too stressed, you may lose control of your feelings and the capacity to act professionally and accordingly.

Consider a time when anxiety has weighed you down. Can it be simple to think clearly or make a logical choice? Probably not. When you become too stressed, your ability to think clearly and correctly evaluate emotions (yours and other people's) becomes endangered.

Emotions are essential pieces of knowledge that inform you about others and yourself. However, in the face of anxiety that takes us from our comfort spot, we can become submerged and lose control.

Together with the capability to handle stress and remain emotionally current, you can learn how to receive disturbing information without allowing it to overturn your ideas and self-control.

You will have the ability to make decisions that enable you to control spontaneous emotions and conduct, handle your emotions in healthy ways, take the initiative, follow through on responsibilities and challenging conditions.

SELF AWARENESS

Self-awareness denotes the capability to identify and comprehend emotions and get a sense of just how one's activities, moods, and other people's feelings take effect. It involves keeping an eye on emotions and discovering different psychological reactions, and having the ability to spot emotions correctly.

Moreover, it includes recognizing how we believe and what we are doing are associated with and consciousness of one's strengths and constraints. Self-awareness is connected with being open to various experiences and fresh ideas, and learning from social interactions.

Stress management is merely the very first step to creating emotional intelligence. The science of attachment suggests your present psychological experience is probably a manifestation of your daily life experience. Your capacity to handle core feelings like anger, despair, anxiety, and pleasure often is based upon the quality and consistency of your everyday life psychological experiences.

In case your principal guardian as a child understood and appreciated your emotions. It is probably that your emotions have become valuable assets as you mature in life. However, suppose your psychological experiences as a child were perplexing, threatening, or debilitating. In that case, you have likely attempted to distance yourself from your emotions.

However, having the ability to relate to your emotions using a moment-to-moment connection with your shifting emotional experience would be the key to knowing how emotion affects your ideas and actions.

Do you experience sentiments that stream, experiencing one feeling after another as your undertakings move from second to second?

Are your emotions followed by substantial vibes you experience in regions like your gut, throat, or chest?

Can you experience emotions and feelings, like anger, despair, fear, and pleasure, every one of which will be evident in facial reactions?

Would you experience extreme feelings that are powerful enough to catch both your attention and that of the others?

Do you center around your feelings? Would they be able to factor into your decisions?

If any event one of these experiences is obscure, you may have "turned down" or "killed" your emotions. To construct EQ and be mentally healthy, you have to reconnect to your heart feelings, take them, and be familiar with them. It is conceivable to accomplish this through the act of Mindfulness.

[150]

Mindfulness is the tradition of knowingly focusing your attention on the current moment without judgment. The culture of mindfulness has origins in Buddhism, but many religions incorporate similar prayer or meditation techniques. Mindfulness helps alter your obsession with a notion toward an appreciation of this minute, your physical and psychological senses, and provides a bigger view on life. Mindfulness calms and streamlines you, which makes you self-aware from the procedure.

SOCIAL AWARENESS

This element of EQ describes interacting well with others. It involves deploying an understanding of ourselves and others' feelings to communicate and socialize with others daily.

Different societal skills include active listening, verbal communication abilities, non-verbal communication abilities, leadership, and connection.

Social consciousness allows you to comprehend and translate the mostly nonverbal prompts others are continuously using to communicate with you. These prompts will enable you to know what others are feeling, just how their emotional state is changing from moment to moment, and what is important to them.

When groups of individuals send out similar nonverbal prompts, you can read and comprehend the team's power dynamics and shared emotional experiences. In summary, you are empathetic and exceptionally comfortable.

Mindfulness Works With Emotional And Social Awareness

To develop social awareness, you have to comprehend the value of mindfulness within the social procedure. In the end, you can not pick up on subtle nonverbal prompts once you are in your head, thinking about anything else, or just zoning on your mobile phone.

Social consciousness requires your presence right now. Though many people pride themselves on the ability to multitask, this usually means you will overlook the subtle emotional changes happening in different people who help you completely understand them.

- You're more likely to enhance your societal goals by placing different ideas aside and focusing on the interaction itself.
- Following the stream of some other individual's emotional reactions is a give-and-take procedure that needs you to look closely at the changes in your moving experience.
- Paying attention to other people does not diminish your self-awareness. By investing time and effort to look closely at other people, you will get insight into your emotional state in addition to your worth and beliefs.
- For instance, if you feel discomfort hearing others say particular views, you will have learned something important about yourself.

RELATIONSHIP MANAGEMENT

Empathy denotes having the ability to comprehend how other people are feeling.

This element of EQ empowers somebody to react appropriately to others based on recognizing their feelings. It enables people to feel power changes, which play a role in all social connections, particularly in office relations.

Empathy involves comprehending power dynamics and how they influence feelings and behavior and correctly perceive situations where power changes come into power.

Working with others is a cycle that starts with emotional mindfulness and your ability to see and comprehend others' experiences. When emotional awareness is in play, you can viably grow additional social/emotional capabilities to make your relationships more fruitful, productive, and satisfying.

Become conscious of how efficiently you use nonverbal communication. It is not possible to prevent sending gestures to other people about what you feel and think. The many muscles on your face, particularly those around the eyes, mouth, nose, and forehead, enable you to express your feelings and see other people's emotional intent. The emotional part of your mind is obviously on, and even if you dismiss its messages, the others will not.

Recognizing the nonverbal messages you send to other people may play a massive role in enhancing your relationships.

Use play and humor to alleviate stress. Comedy, laughter, and drama are natural antidotes to stress. They decrease your desires and help you keep things in context. Giggling brings your sensory system into balance, lessening uneasiness, quieting you down, massaging your head, and makes you more empathic.

Figure out how to view conflict as an opportunity to develop closer relationships with others. Strife and differences are unavoidable in human connections. Two individuals can not possibly have the very same needs, opinions, and expectations always. However, that shouldn't be a terrible thing.

Resolving conflict in healthy, constructive ways may reinforce trust between individuals. When a dispute is not perceived as threatening or sanctioning, it boosts freedom, imagination, and security in relationships.

MOTIVATION

Motivation, when regarded as a part of EQ, describes inherent ambition.

Inherent motivation usually means that an individual is driven to satisfy personal needs and goals instead of being motivated by external rewards like money, fame, and recognition. Intrinsically motivated individuals also undergo a state of "flow" by being immersed in the action.

They are more inclined to be action-oriented and purpose-driven. Such people typically need for accomplishment and find ways to be better. They are also more likely to be dedicated and also take the first step.

DEVELOPING EMOTIONAL INTELLIGENCE

It is apparent that we are all emotionally smart, but we have to take more time to self-assess and operate on our feelings. Just like anything, it takes practice, but even little steps can make a difference. Much as you'd frequently work out your biceps or some other muscular for that matter, you will need to exercise working on your competencies so that they can improve.

Ironically, once we examine leaders in a number of the most prosperous businesses, it is apparent that each one of these leaders possesses and demonstrates elevated levels of all of the vital elements of emotional intelligence. It is important to remember these are a variety of skills.

Overall, women generally have greater emotional empathy: sensing how a person is at the moment and managing relationships between groups and people. The link between emotional intelligence and leadership is that there are gaps between women and men within this realm, but as individuals develop, they pick up skills from the field they require.

Emotional intelligence is a theory researchers came up with around the 1980s and 90s to describe why smart people frequently do dumb things. The argument went that in the same manner, your overall intelligence quotient (IQ) is a measurement of your ability to process information made available to you and make sound conclusions. Your emotional intelligence (EQ) is the capacity to process emotions. That of others' along with yours, come to sound decisions.

Some people have a remarkably high IQ but low EQ--believe your nutty professor can not fit his socks or does not find the purpose of having a hair cut. Other individuals have unbelievably high EQ but low IQ--imagine the road hustler who can not even spell his name but somehow speaks you into lending him the shirt off your back.

[155]

Psychologists who study emotional intelligence occasionally assert it is even more significant than general intellect. This statement is contentious at best. For starters, measuring emotional intelligence is hard, maybe impossible. Almost all of the stuff is subjective.

However, because emotional intelligence is not as secure as overall intellect is, IQ is more difficult to change. However, EQ is something that you can work on and build as a muscle or a skill and observe it grow, like the flower in your garden.

So, essentially, no matter how smart you are, you do not have any excuse. The significance of creating emotional intelligence cannot be overemphasized.

Below are a few ways to begin doing this.

EXERCISE SELF-AWARENESS

Like many psychological things, you can not get better until you know what they are. When you lack self-awareness, attempting to handle your emotions is like sitting at a tiny boat with no sail in the sea of your emotions, completely at the whim of these currents of anything occurring moment by moment. You don't have any idea where you're going or how to get there. The only thing you do is shout and shout for assistance.

Self-awareness entails understanding your behavior on three levels:

- What you are doing,
- The way you are feeling about it, and
- What don't you understand about yourself?

Understanding What You Are Doing.

You would think this should be relatively straightforward. However, the simple truth is that in the 21st century, the majority of us do not even understand what we are doing half of the time. We are on auto-pilot. Check email, message boy/girlfriend, assess Instagram, view YouTube, check email, text spouse.

Eliminating distractions in life--such as, you know, turning off your telephone today and then and engaging with the world around you is a beautiful first step to self-awareness. Locating areas of solitude and silence. While these are possibly frightening, they are essential for our emotional wellbeing. Other kinds of distraction involve work, TV, drugs/alcohol, video games, cross-stitching, arguing with folks on the net, among others.

Schedule time in your day to escape from them. Do your morning commute with no podcast or music. Just consider your life. Consider how you're feeling. Set aside 10 minutes from the morning to meditate. Delete social networking off your phone for a week. You may often be surprised by what happens to you.

We use these distractions to prevent many uncomfortable feelings. Therefore removing distractions and focusing on how you feel with no may sometimes show some frightening troubles. But eliminating distractions is critical since it gets us to another level.

Understand What You Are Feeling

Initially, once you genuinely listen to the way you feel, it may frighten you. You may come to realize you are often really pretty miserable or that you are mad at a lot of people in your lifetime.

[157]

You may understand that there is a good deal of stress going on. The whole phone dependency thing is only a method to numb and guard yourself out of this anxiety continuously.

It is vital at this stage not to judge the feelings that come up.

You will be tempted to say anything like, "what's wrong with me? However, making it worse. No matter what emotion is, there's a great reason to be there, even if you do not recall what that reason is. Therefore do not be too hard on your own.

MANAGE YOUR LANGUAGE.

Deliberately become a more influential communicator at work. Emotionally intelligent individuals will, in general, utilize more explicit expressions to help pass on insufficiencies, and they, at that point, promptly work to handle them.

Had a "not-so-good" encounter with the boss? What made it so bad, and what do you do to fix it next time? As soon as you can pinpoint what is happening, you now have a greater likelihood of resolving the issue instead of merely brooding on it and generating negative emotions.

Understanding Your Emotions

As soon as you see all of the uncomfortable things you feel, you will start to judge where your anger resides.

For example, I get very touchy about being upset. I get irrationally mad when I am attempting to talk. When the person I am talking to is not focused, I take it personally. While sometimes it's just them being impolite, sometimes stuff happens, and that I wind up seeming like a complete douchebag. I can not stand moving two seconds with no word I say being respected.

These are some of the emotional issues you might be dealing with, and you can only react accordingly if you are aware of them.

Now, only being self-aware is not adequate in and of itself. An individual needs to have the ability to handle their feelings also.

When you can handle and lower your negative emotions, you are not as likely to get overpowered. It sounds a little too easy, right? Try this: When somebody is bothering you, do not be hurry into concluding you know why.

Instead, allow yourself to examine the situation in diverse ways. Try to view issues objectively, which means you don't get touchy or vexed all the time. Practice mindfulness on the job, and see how your approach changes.

CHANNELING YOUR EMOTIONS WELL

Individuals who think that emotions would be the be-all-end-all of lifestyle frequently find ways to "control" their feelings. You can not. You may respond to them.

Emotions are only the signs that tell us to look closely at something. We can then choose whether that something is significant and pick the most appropriate plan of action in fixing it or not.

There is no such thing as "appropriate" or "inappropriate" emotions that there are just "appropriate" and "inappropriate" responses to your own emotions.

Anger may be a harmful emotion should you misdirect it and harm yourself or others in the procedure. However, it is sometimes a fantastic emotion to use to fight injustices and shield others or yourself.

Joy could be an excellent emotion when shared by people that you like when something incredible happens. However, it can be a dreadful emotion if it is derived from damaging others.

This is the act of handling your emotions: recognizing precisely what you feel, determining whether that's a suitable emotion to your circumstance, and behaving accordingly.

The entire purpose of this would be to have the ability to channel your feelings to what psychologists call "goal-oriented" behavior.

PRODUCE HEALTHIER RELATIONSHIPS

Everything we have covered so many deals with directing and handling emotions within yourself. Nevertheless, the entire purpose of creating emotional intelligence should finally be to cultivate healthy relationships in your daily life.

Healthy relationships, like intimate relationships, comfortable relationships, and other forms of relationships, start with understanding and regarding each other's feelings.

You do so by linking and empathizing with other people, by both listening to other people and discussing yourself honestly with other people, in other words, through exposure.

To empathize with somebody does not necessarily imply entirely understanding them, but accepting them as they are, even before you know them. You learn how to appreciate their presence and treat them as their end instead of a means for somebody different. You accept their pain as your pain, as our collective pain.

Relationships get us from our minds and to the world. They make us understand we are part of something much bigger and considerably more complicated than merely ourselves. Relationships are, in the end, the way we show our value.

INSTILL EMOTIONS WITH VALUES

Back in the 90s, emotional intelligence was the major buzzword in psychology. CEOs and team lead read books and attended numerous retreats on emotional intelligence to inspire their workforces.

Therapists attempted to instill more emotional awareness in their clients to help them handle their lifestyles. Parents have been admonished to nurture emotional intelligence in their kids to prepare them for a transforming, emotionally-oriented world.

A good deal of this form of thinking misses the point, nevertheless. And that's that emotional intelligence is meaningless without orienting your self-worth.

You may have the most emotionally smart CEO on earth, but when she uses her abilities to inspire her workers to market products produced by exploiting bad people or ruining the world, how is being emotionally smart a virtue?

A dad might teach his child the tenets of emotional intelligence, but by failing to teach him the values of respect and honesty, he could become a ruthless, lying little boy. However, an emotionally smart one!

Conmen are highly emotionally smart. They know emotions very well, both in themselves and notably others. However, they wind up using that knowledge to control others for their personal gain. They respect themselves above all and at the cost of others. Things get nasty once you appreciate little outside of your self.

Finally, we are always picking what we appreciate, whether we understand it or not. Also, our emotions will execute those values by inspiring our behavior somehow.

To live the life you really want to live, you need to be clear about what you truly value because that is where your mental energy will be led.

Understanding what you truly appreciate, not precisely what you say you appreciate, is possibly the most emotionally smart skill you can develop.

EXERCISE EMPATHY

Paying attention to nonverbal and verbal prompts may provide you a priceless understanding of your coworkers' or customers' feelings. Practice focusing on others and seeing things from their perspective, even if it's only for a brief moment. Make firm statements and don't excuse improper behavior. However, they help remind one that everybody has their difficulties.

KNOW YOUR STRESSORS

Take stock and identify what stresses you and be more aggressive to have less of it in your life. If you realize that assessing your job email before bed will drive you into a tailspin, leave it for your morning hours. Even better, make it when you arrive in the workplace.

RECOVER FROM MISFORTUNE

Everybody encounters difficulties. How you react to these issues, set you up for progress or put you on the path to full emergency mode. You realize that positive reasoning will benefit you. To help you to skip back from a problematic situation, practice positivity as opposed to whining. What did you learn in the present condition? Carry out objective inquiries to know what you can learn from the challenge.

Emotional intelligence can advance as long as you have the desire to improve it. Every person, question, or situation stood up to is a superb learning opportunity to check your EQ. It requires preparing; however, you can start receiving the rewards immediately.

Having a higher level of emotional intelligence will work well for you in your office relationships and other life areas.

MENTAL INTELLIGENCE IN THE WORKPLACE

Human resources managers search for several features within an employee when they're interviewing. For instance, the candidate ought to be trustworthy. They must have experience and knowledge in the job he or she will do. The interviewee must be a fast learner and fit nicely on a team and possess a development mindset.

An employer might also be keeping a lookout for general intellect, indications of rational thinking, as well as ambition. However,

[163]

along with this, employers could be smart to search for signs of emotional intelligence.

There are several advantages to having emotionally smart employees. Emotional intelligence has turned out to make people work with each other. In reality, it's about how folks work within their relationships and with themselves.

Someone might be highly competent in all places; however, if they cannot get along with co-workers, superiors, and customers and are not capable of self-motivation. This worker might be no good for your company. So what advantages of emotional intelligence are there to enjoy in a workplace?

How can a supervisor, administrator, or company owner gain from highly emotionally intelligent employees? Why does hiring with this particular top quality benefit the company? Here is how:

CHANGES CAN BE MADE EASILY

It's significant for an organization not to stay stale. By continually zeroing in on self and organizational fitted improvement, a business will undoubtedly encounter change.

Even though employees probably realize that changes inside their organization depend on what is required or what is best for the business. In any case, they may not generally greet it wholeheartedly. We, as a people, have consistently battled with change.

Nonetheless, employees with high emotional intelligence change effectively and, as a rule, grasp the change and develop in line with the organizational objectives. This is a critical character characteristic that can be infectious among the team.

BETTER TEAM-WORK

It is indisputable that workers can do the job in a group when they have greater emotional intelligence. Individuals with greater EQ communicate better with group members than people who are not in tune with their wisdom.

They examine thoughts and are available to recommendations from colleagues. They are not as slanted to totally assume responsibility for a circumstance and "handle everything" freely without considering others.

These workers are more inclined to trust their colleagues and appreciate their thoughts and input. They're respectful and considerate as the team works together. This is a perfect situation for a company.

BETTER WORKING ENVIRONMENT

Morale boosting is among many advantages of emotional intelligence at work. Whenever you've got an office filled with a team that gets together and respects one another, the business culture is guaranteed to be considerably more powerful.

Unexpectedly, the office also becomes an area of pleasure. Not only will employees appreciate the job they're doing, but they'll also delight in the individuals with whom they get it done.

Suppose you want to promote a feeling of teamwork and encouragement in your office. In that case, you should make an effort to create your break space a more enjoyable place, stocked with refreshments along with wholesome snacks. Within this environment, co-workers will delight in one another's company and share thoughts or future tendencies over a cup of workplace java. This produces a strong sense of teamwork and encouragement within the office.

If a workplace is situated in a crowded town, you need to turn the break room into an area for co-workers to convene. For example, taking strides to get your break room pleasurable provides workers a place to locate coffee and tasty snacks without even leaving the construction.

Office supervisors will observe that this is finally reflected in additional business areas, such as client services. This exemplary customer service is going to lead to happy clients. That is a win-win for everybody.

EMPATHY

Perhaps the best advantage of emotional intelligence, both inside the working environment and in one's very own life, is the capacity to keep up and show empathy for fellow humans. Empathy allows an individual to associate with others on an emotional level.

This can be an extraordinary advantage to a business when their workers show empathy. Compassion can be imparted to a customer that missed an installment because of a challenging situation.

Empathy can be shared with a colleague managing a personal crisis and requiring somebody to cover their obligations. Compassion can likewise be shown to leadership for the choices they need to make daily.

Empathy helps us associate with others. By showing compassion, an employee helps connect the work environment and improve the organization's morale and, by and large, reputation. This is a precious advantage. It's additionally, sadly, not typically teachable expertise.

SELF-AWARENESS

Among the advantages of emotional intelligence in workers is that it helps them understand their strengths and flaws. These workers can make comments and use them favorably to enhance and grow as a person.

Many times, supervisors will encounter defensiveness when providing constructive and necessary comments to a worker. This alone could lead to frustration and a block in productivity. Another difficulty leaders face is workers not understanding their particular constraints.

While emotionally intelligent people understand themselves and what they can achieve at a particular number of hours. Others are somewhat more inclined to overpromise and underdeliver.

Workers with high emotional intelligence can learn from constructive criticism and be conscious of what they can do. These are valuable tools.

BETTER MANAGEMENT

A leader has the right to anticipate his or her workers to meet deadlines. Based upon the business, this may mean the difference between getting the dime or going hungry.

In less tumultuous companies, it may minimally trigger frustration and a split between employer and employee. Individuals with greater emotional intelligence can manage their time better, maximizing their productivity.

Among the most significant advantages of emotional intelligence at work is a leader does not believe they need to micromanage their workers. By employing individuals demonstrating a high emotional intelligence, specific projects will be finished, and deadlines will be met.

It is only that these folks understand how to prioritize jobs and have them completed in time. What a fantastic feeling!

PROFESSIONAL RELATIONSHIPS

Among the advantages of emotional intelligence is knowing other people. Members of staff with higher EQ understand what makes others tick. They could withstand what others enjoy and do not like.

This helps a connection, professional or otherwise, grow and grow into a solid, strong one. Possessing high emotional intelligence also enables an individual to be quite tuned in to your body language and facial expressions of the people they are communicating with.

This is a valuable skill in business and private life too. Having the ability to "read" individuals correctly allows you to interact better and speak appropriately.

You can identify what others are thinking and feeling rather than merely the words they are saying. "It is not what you say; it is the way you say it." It's a thought process that means very much to individuals with high emotional intelligence. By communicating nicely, it develops relationships with customers, co-workers, and leaders.

BETTER SELF-CONTROL

Individuals with high emotional intelligence understand how to deal with challenges in business conditions. However, there are bound to be situations that don't necessarily feel comfortable in business, especially for an individual in a leadership position.

A challenging situation could be involving an unhappy customer. When dealing with unhappy customers, it means staying positive and calm, even if you don't always feel like that on the inside.

A challenging situation could be exceptional in that your boss is unhappy with your job. This produces a feeling of unease and humiliation.

It might be a rough conversation with a poor, either between disciplinary action or getting fired. In situations such as these, an individual has to be firm yet calm. A challenging situation might even be a co-worker posing the challenge of providing information used against you.

This usually means keeping an understanding of the head and staying calm. If an employee can avoid an emotional outburst and remain calm in situations like these, it may be better.

Individuals with a high EQ know that behaving negatively, provocatively, or absurdly will escalate a situation. These workers can quickly practice restraint and show their emotions when it is proper, and even then, do this in a controlled way.

MOTIVATION

Emotionally Intelligent people are optimistic and are continually working towards a target, whether professional, personal or even both. These individuals possess an increased mindset, and they persevere regardless of the challenges they face.

These workers are not inspired by external forces but instead are driven by their inner vision. Individuals with high EQ work hard for the satisfaction of knowing they finished the work successfully.

They will work for you, plus they do not give up easily. It is essential to be aware that those workers, while frequently appreciative and worthy of pay increases and bonuses, are quick to be turned off with imitation or little rewards.

Their job is equally important and is founded on merit alone. It is essential to retain these valuable staff by keeping them happy and making their lives simpler. If your workplace is located at a bustling place, you must bring these benefits to keep them inspired.

There are several ways to make office life easier in busy and highly active cities by providing your workers ways to refresh during the day.

LEADERSHIP CAPABILITIES

Organizations are continually looking for quality managers, as they expected. These managers create significant differences in productivity and profitability, allowing every worker to feel respected and appreciated.

It is reasonable, then, that company owners and human resources managers would seek out talents with high emotional intelligence. These workers have compassion for others' feelings and conditions.

They have practical knowledge and experience of human character. As a result of this, they have a positive influence on their subordinates. They may be nurturing another business.

These leaders can inspire workers. Individuals working for leaders who have high emotional intelligence are encouraged to do their best since their best is excellent for the organization and their boss. Leaders with these qualities can create a massive impact on the business culture.

TIME TO SHAKE THINGS UP

Many businesses are still playing catch up on the significance of hiring for emotional intelligence. This is not a fad that is taken shape entirely. As a result of this, other businesses might not own a group that feels appreciated. Employing a new talent with high emotional intelligence can help your business stick out among its rivals.

These businesses may struggle with teams that don't work nicely together and lack motivation. This is an edge to get over your insightful competitors, which may be extremely valuable.

It is common knowledge the type of team businesses wish to have; powerful, cohesive, go-getters work nicely together. However, often, these firms stop at only considering the group. This dream-team includes dream-employees.

By focusing on the team, leaders may gain that advantage over their competitors who are still thinking about getting their workers to operate well together.

Now that you are clued to the pros of emotional intelligence and understand it's high quality and valuable advantage for a worker, what do you do about it?

Start with what you have at the moment. Have a look at a present talent. Who exhibits the traits listed above?

Who gets along with all sorts of people, shows compassion, and continuously works well in a group? In case you have not, think about leadership positions for workers like these. When picking an employee to lead a specific team or finish a particular project, resist the need to choose the employee with the most expertise.

Instead, identify the one which displays high emotional intelligence. Next, alter your interview procedure. You will still have to include questions concerning technical problems, education, and expertise.

However, add to those questions, which have scenarios where you would require a greater emotional intelligence to succeed. Please, pay attention to their responses and think about these when determining whether to employ them.

Now you know the advantages of emotional intelligence at work, it'll be simple to recognize those who show it and the people who struggle. The main thing is you are one step ahead of enhancing the office environment for your business.

DEVELOPING EMOTIONAL INTELLIGENCE IN KIDS/TEENS

If you could teach a set of abilities to each kid on the planet, what could it be? Imagine if it may be something which would bring intellect and empathy to decision-making, reduce or put an end to violence, engraft within humankind a push towards kindness, compassion and build relationships that connect, treat, nurture and flourish individuals that are inside them?

Emotional intelligence can do so, and when we can teach it to each kid on Earth, by the time the entire world was in their own hands, we would be living in an incredible one.

The matter is, we do not have to instruct it to each kid on earth. We have to teach only one at a time.

Emotional intelligence entails recognizing and handling feelings appropriately in ourselves and our relationships and knowing what others feel.

The brain's emotional centers are closely linked to the regions involved in cognitive learning. Therefore it is not surprising that there's a plethora of research emphasizing the importance of emotional intelligence for achievement.

Assisting children in creating emotional intelligence increases their odds of succeeding in college, job, and lifestyle. A recent study discovered that the preschoolers that had been considered by their teachers as emotionally intelligent, as measure by how they help others, openness to discuss, and a capability to solve their peer issues -- were, by age 25, prone to have graduated from school, maintain the full-time occupation, less inclined to have been detained and not as willing to maintain public housing or to a public housing waitlist than pupils who were not as socially capable.

The analysis results were independent of the consequences of poverty, race, being born to adolescent parents, family stress, and local crime.

Being emotionally intelligent is your ability to become present or conscious with your emotions, which requires a specific degree of awareness. Naturally, teenagers are still growing portions of the brain, which may inhibit their capacity to become aware.

The prefrontal cortex, the portion of the brain that governs logic and reason, is still growing. For the large part, because adolescents lack a fully developed prefrontal cortex, they are sometimes impulsive and emotional and lack some level of emotional intelligence.

Many times, teens need guidance about what to do with their emotions. Even though they often like to act independently. For many adolescents, emotions come on strong, and they can not have the resources to handle these feelings. In more awful case situations, a youngster may go to liquor or drugs to manage their emotions. In other scenarios, a teenager might distance themselves from believing and possibly even become miserable.

In high school, academic success is the main focus. It's easy to forget that teenagers will need to continue to grow and develop their emotional intelligence. Teens using a high level of emotional intelligence can better control their feelings and behavior when things do not go their way.

This, at that point, makes them more joyful, more transparent as crystal, and more deferential of others. Understudies with a high EQ will, in general, perform better in school. They tune in, learn, stay motivated, and coexist with classmates and instructors.

When it comes to our kids, we are the ones who can fuel their trip, and constructing their emotional intelligence is a sure way to get this done. We can not pick their temperament, and we can not choose their personality, but we can model it.

Here is how:

BOND OVER ENTERTAINMENT.

Novels and films present perfect opportunities to talk to teens about feelings and behavior. Suppose you and your young person have read a similar book or saw the same movie, for instance, The Black Panther. Use these anecdotal characters to have an exchange. Discussion about a character's intentions and objectives. Ask your teen, "What do you truly think he is feeling?" And "For what reason would you accept he did this?

Likewise, after seeing a movie together at the cinema, on your way home, ask your child why somebody was mad, frustrated, sad, or excited. These discussions help children become used to talking and thinking about why folks behave the way they do and how they may have responded differently. Speaking about literary characters makes it much easier for teenagers to be mentally eloquent when discussing their emotions. That is the entire idea.

OWN YOUR IMPERFECTION

Be real and own your imperfection. After all, you are of this world and not some angel. It is incredible, and you are the only one on earth that does humans precisely the way you do. Embracing your imperfection can help your kids to adopt theirs. Permit yourself to fall flat, miss the point, and give it to yourself while you are at it.

You will have off days, off minutes, and on occasion, you will make things up. It is a part of living and about the world. Whenever you do, let your children see you have this, and if they come to you to discuss their own mistakes, then be thankful for the chance to strengthen the relationship. Nothing feels better than somebody accepting us when we are not so deserving of the embrace.

ASK YOUR TEENS QUESTIONS

During family outings, household rides, or at the dinner table, the "What will you do if...? style of questioning gets your adolescent considering ways to react to unique scenarios. Pose inquiries that incite them to act with more emotional intelligence "How will you respond on the off chance that you saw somebody being tormented at school?

Or should I blame you for something that you did not do?" Asking such questions when emotions are not running high allows your child to develop tips about the best way to react and offer you some thoughts of your own.

TEACH AND SHOW THEM HOW TO LISTEN

Listening is vital to developing emotionally intelligent youngsters. People naturally gravitate towards those that listen to them. The attraction is more than magical. To teach these to young people, reflect on what they said to you. Ask a question like "What you mean is...?" Or Affirmations like, "I understand what you are saying..."

Avoid all forms of distraction when they are talking to you and demand the same. Create time to be with them fully in person and with your full attention. This way, they can learn how the listening thing works.

TEACH KINDNESS

Most parents will state that kindness is vital, but children do not get this message, presuming that grades would be the main point. Even though grade levels are critical, compassion is at the center of social competence, relationships, and link.

Advising them to be caring is something. However, allowing them to see you are kind to yourself, to them, to individuals that you know, to outsiders, that is the place where the enchantment is.

ROLE PLAY

Charades is a cool game for families to find out about and safely convey a range of emotions. To perform charades: An individual pulls a slip of paper out of a container and gently reads the phrase written there. At that point, the individual demonstrations it out to others to figure what it is. You can play in gatherings when a group wins if one individual guesses correctly in a fixed timeframe.

It works because it removes words and focuses on the body, facial expressions, and gestures. This is good for the emotions of a young person. Create your classes. Matters at a birthday celebration. How to react when you are angry. Creatures. Sports. Your creative mind is your cutoff.

Often we do not know or believe we act in particular or say something. However, seeing someone act it out and other people guessing it right in a game might be the change we need for our emotional intelligence.

FEEL FREE TO DISAGREE

Brokering different points of view effectively is a significant part of keeping relationships and keeping a sense of self in these relationships. Allow them to disagree with you occasionally without attempting to change their position. "I understand where you are coming from; however, I see it in another way."

Understanding someone does not mean that you agree with them. This means that you respect their right to their view, and you would like to keep the relationship and dialog open. Individuals will always appreciate those who honor their opinions, even if they disagree.

ANGER MANAGEMENT

Not only are you able to use stories as a launchpad to go over feelings, but you might also get books that tackle feelings right. For preadolescents and adolescents, anger is among the most challenging emotions they have to manage.

A fantastic book to help them know how to deal with and handle this raw emotion can go a very long way. Teens talk about their particular techniques to put on self-esteem, manage stress, and cope with anger. Read it with them, or hand it to your kid to learn useful hints on dealing with all the preteen and adolescent years' emotional roller coaster.

PLAY THE "MAYBE" GAME

Recognizing why others act the way they do or show empathy is a vital EQ skill. To practice your compassion skills, play with the "Maybe" game. See somebody raging by the roadside because the traffic light stopped them? Everybody in the car may have a chance at imagining why this individual is feeling so poorly. "Maybe" she's late for work," "maybe" she did not have a good night's rest." "Maybe" she is an extraterrestrial and can not stand how earthlings drive." It can be light-hearted. Occasionally learning and talking about feelings can be enjoyable.

What's more, when someone in the house is irritable, the "maybe" game does something unique for sorting out the reasoning behind bad reactions. "Maybe you are so angry about your assignments as you will need something to eat," "Maybe you are giving the silent treatment because I did not clean the dishes up when you requested."

DO NOT SUPPRESS THEIR EMOTIONS.

All emotions have motives for being there, and it is OK to feel each one of these. The further these feelings are denied expression, the more those feelings will probably push for expression. The longer it takes to express these feelings, the more delicate it becomes.

Give your kids the room to sense their emotions without attempting to alter or talk them out of how they feel. Letting the feelings come out is the key to letting them go in the long run. When emotions are refused expression and buried, their way is blocked. This can lead to depression, general anger to the world, fiery explosion once the pent up energy is completed without being stifled.

REFRAIN FROM USING "SHAMING" AS PUNISHMENT

If punishment entails shaming, smacking, and crying, how the child will learn how to everyone around them on the receiving end. We will have bad days when we lose it; well, that is okay, we are all human.

However, when shaming becomes constant, it affects young ones and how they see themselves and respond to the world.

Shame never changes anyone for the better. It is vital to have boundaries. However, it is also important to show our children how to shield them with elegance without undermining anyone else. People, our children inclusive, will always give you more of everything you need and desire if their bounds are retained and if they feel respected, liked, and valued.

ENCOURAGE FRIENDSHIP

An essential part of emotional intelligence is reading and reacting to relationships. The conclusion about who we allow closure is always ours to create. Inspire your kid, with no judgment, to review their friendships regarding the way they are in these relationships. What do they get from the company? Would they have the option to feel significantly better or more lamentable without it? Does this draw out the absolute best or most noticeably awful in them?

These are not simple things to consider or to respond to. However, the sooner they could create this mindset and possess their capability to pick the people they want as friends, the happier they will be.

When relationships feel awful, it's generally because they are. If those relationships do, the harm is if it is accepted as proof of a personal deficiency on their part. It is not. Let your children understand this. If folks maltreat other people, they are generally driven by their particular history and hurts.

That hurt can be infectious. It is not the responsibility of other people to assume liability for someone else's healing. We should not get in the way of this, but we do not have to be a goal for anybody else's pain or disorder.

Urge your kids to review their conduct with an open heart. When there's nothing that they could change to make the relationship feel better, it is probably that the friendship does not deserve them.

Enable them to maintain the friendship should they feel the need. The longer you struggle with their companies, the longer they will shield them, which may tie up the power they will need to learn more about the friendship and what it implies to them.

In contrast, if you empower them as those who possess the best choice about whether or not to remain, they will feel respected and do the right thing. Being alone is not a sign of the popularity or lack of. It is the contrast between leaving relationships that don't merit them and finding those that do.

ACCEPT NATURAL APOLOGIES

Making children apologize too fast and over everything wrong might mean they have no idea why they apologize. Compassion is at the core of an expression of remorse and will be passing up a constrained one. Apologies do not automatically cure a relationship, and they do not, by default, fix everything. Children must know this.

Or maybe, ask how they see the circumstance and accept someone else may view the condition. When there's something they have missed, then gently point it out. Instead of telling them to apologize, inquire what courageous steps they may choose to make it up to the other person. It may not necessarily be a verbal or written apology. If they have hurt a sibling, then they may believe that a cuddle will do the magic.

If they have inadvertently pushed somebody on the sports area, it may be saying, 'Are you really okay? I didn't intend to hurt you' Do not disgrace them, notwithstanding, permit them to be a hero of the situation. There are generally different sides to every story. Validate theirs and encourage them to realize the full effect of whatever it's they have done.

[182]

The more disgraced they feel, the harder it will be to claim whatever they have fouled up and make it right. The concept is to nurture them to be reactive whenever they get things wrong, not defensive.

EMOTIONAL INTELLIGENCE IN LEADERSHIP

The specialized abilities that got you your first advancement on the job might probably not be enough to guarantee the next.

If you aspire to occupy a leadership role, there is an emotional aspect you need to consider. Managers set the pace of their firms. Lacking emotional intelligence could bring about a radical plunge.

The abilities conceived of Emotional intelligence make models of favored conduct. They can be summarized as self-awareness, social awareness, and self-management.

For example, suppose you can not communicate with your team or collaborate with others as a leader. In that case, you are not fit to occupy a leadership position.

Being self-aware when in an administrative role implies having an understanding of your qualities and shortcomings. Team leaders who direct themselves barely obnoxiously assault others, generalize people or undermine their worth.

Self-guideline covers a leaders' adaptability and obligation to individual responsibility.

Motivation is another element a good leader needs to possess. Leaders who are highly motivated work towards their goals and have a high standard for their work quality.

Emotional Intelligence helps you as a leader to coach and mentor others. There is an ability to develop people in your team, challenge others who are lacking behind, give constructive feedback, and most importantly, listen.

Another aspect of leadership, most leaders shy away from is conflict resolution. Unaddressed conflicts might drain the team's performance, and there will be side talks causing the organization to lose productive time.

Humor is another element used by emotionally intelligent leaders to elevate the mood of their colleagues or teammates. For example, a good joke or creative play on words can win over a skeptical customer.

As a leader with emotional intelligence, you can also determine in which situations humor can be used as you need to find a balance between serious work and lightheadedness.

Emotional intelligence in leadership gives the ability to know and recognize the dynamics in play in your organization. You can understand the feeling and perspectives of your coworkers.

These characteristics seem simple, but they inform how well a leader makes decisions, tolerates or works under pressure, and manages time.

Here are examples of CEOs who used their emotional intelligence and the result reflected in their businesses.

JEFF BEZOS: CEO OF AMAZON

JEFF BEZOS: CEO of Amazon

Amazon fulfillment centers have been berated for harsh working conditions. Bezos has reacted by saying, ``Anecdote of "callous management practices do not describe the Amazon or amazonian I work with every day."

We don't have the foggiest idea of how incensed Bezos may have been. However, he was genuinely experienced and savvied with his reaction.

URSULA BURN;

Ursula Burn;

She succeeded previous CEO Anne Mulcahy as the first woman-to-woman CEO exchange in Fortune 500. She additionally guided xeroxing out of a near chapter 11 scenario.

Mulcahy wrote:

"Earlier in her career, she didn't have a good poker face. All her emotions were visible, and that's a big thing for a CEO because everybody is looking at her. As chief executive, you have to set the right tone consciously, and Ursula worked to develop it".

With time, Burns began to get it and emerge as a self-confident leader who first put the company's interest.

ELON MUSK, CEO TESLA AND SPACEX

In response to a recent claim that Tesla has incurred 30% more employees injuries than the industry standard, Musk committed to personal accountability in an email to employees.

He shows that it makes him extremely upset when a worker is hurt constructing vehicles and earnestly focuses on their security.

"This is what all managers at Tesla got... At Tesla, we lead from the frontline, not from a safe and comfortable ivory tower. Managers must always put their team's safety above their own"

Actions are more potent than words. Musk offers to work alongside factory workers to understand their perspective. This shows he really cared.

SATYA NADELLA, CEO OF MICROSOFT

Rather than reprimanding the specialists who dealt with the day, he sent them an email;

"Keep pushing, and know that I am with you... The key is to keep learning and improving."

The email showed his employee that he has their back, and by encouraging them, they learn from their mistakes.

JACK WELCH, FORMER CHAIRMAN AND CEO OF GENERAL ELECTRIC.

Rather than terminating Welch, the executives showed empathy. Transforming costly missteps into both an exercise and a chance to advance. The bombed project brought about a superior product.

[186]

INDRA NOOYI, CEO OF PEPSICO

Through her extraordinary presentation of appreciation, she allied with her executives in a genuine and profoundly close-to-home manner that caused her to build dedication and resolve.

ALAN MULALLY, FORMER CEO OF FORDS

He wrote handwritten notes to the employees praising them for their work.

Emotional intelligence characteristics are the most admirable of human organizations, and these CEOs use emotional intelligence to expand their businesses.

THE EMOTIONALLY INTELLIGENT MANAGER

Emotionally intelligent managers know a lot about their feelings and activities. They are mindful of the emotions of others. They are not only ready to tune in to the worries of others, but they can interpret, even peacefully, the feelings sold out through outward appearances or non-verbal communication.

HOW BUSINESS MANAGERS DEPLOY EMOTIONAL INTELLIGENCE DAILY

During a phone call;

Your client expresses anger about their partnership with you. You have also come to find out their organization is laying off staff, and she is in charge of selecting her team member to go. Instead of reacting to her demeanor, you can best reschedule the call.

During a project review;

During a project you put together, you received professional criticism about how the project could have been done. Instead of feeling deflated, see it as a way to improve on future projects.

Leadership requires authority over the group's vision; however, it should be entwined with putting their necessities first. Those acknowledgments provide more productive workers, create happier and effective managers.

Work environment stress might be inaccessible; however, leaders with emotional intelligence oversee it better and don't allow it to burn through them. They can separate between work life and everyday life.

Benefits Of EQ In Leadership

General company culture:

Emotional intelligence-driven leaders encourage more robust relationships and open communication, which moves such a company's culture to what it ought to be.

High Performance Driven Results:

Employees whose emotions are valued and not subjected to their bosses' negative and unfiltered emotions perform better.

In conclusion, All in all, When members of staff feel regarded, comprehended, and esteemed, you have established a climate they would not have any desire to leave.

To be compelling, business leaders should have a strong comprehension of their feelings and activities for others around them. The better a leader identifies and works with others, the more effective he becomes.

BENEFITS OF EMOTIONAL INTELLIGENCE

Ever wondered why you took some steps or made some decisions? The person to blame is your emotional intelligence. Our emotional intelligence influences the nature of our lives since it impacts our conduct and connections.

WHAT ARE THE BENEFIT OF EMOTIONAL INTELLIGENCE

Better Communications

As humans, we have different emotions and feelings such as jealousy, fear, anger, happiness, love, and others. Emotional intelligence will help to express these feelings. How we understand our emotions, and that of others will determine how well we channel these emotions.

Ability To Deal With Change;

Not everyone likes or appreciates Change, but emotional intelligence gives you the required tools to deal with it and adapt accordingly.

Productivity;

People with high emotional intelligence help solve problems and manage conflicts efficiently.

Subsequently, they are more productive in their career and empower others to do likewise.

Allows For Better Teamwork;

Emotional intelligent people are equipped with good communication, trust each other and value each other's input. That is, when someone makes a suggestion, they can respond productively and positively.

Compassion;

Showing empathy fortifies relationships, decrease pressure and tension, and increases understanding in a period where fulfilling objectives and time constraints are esteemed more than individuals.

Culture;

Cultivating a climate where everybody regards and trusts each other helps build a culture of help and shared advantages.

Self Awareness;

They are available to criticism that will help them improve. They are likewise more mindful and touchy to the emotions of others.

Self Control;

Whether dealing with a nagging boss or an unsatisfied customer, people with high emotional intelligence know that acting irrationally will only make matters get out of hand. They are equipped to practice restraint in a controlled manner.

It Gives You Or Your Business A Leap;

Being or having an emotionally intelligent person as part of your team gives your work or business a boost. That is, you are aware of areas that need improvement and ready to take it. This gives you a leap ahead of your competitors.

Emotional Intelligence Can Make Your Career;

It is a fantastic method to center your energy one way with an enormous outcome.

Emotional Intelligence Can Save Your life;

Bottled emotions before long turn into the awkward mayhem of pressure, stress, and nervousness.

Untackled emotions put a strain on the mind and the body. Your Emotional intelligence helps make stress manageable by enabling you to identify and deal with such situations before things get out of hand.

It Helps In Addressing Issues Privately;

As an Emotional intelligence person, you are aware of how to respond to issues.

For example, a junior colleague mistakenly erases a vital document. It is best to address him privately to shame or kill his self-esteem. It further shows how matured you are.

It Boosts Confidence

Emotional intelligence gives the boost needed to share opinions and listen to others without feeling hurt when your idea is off or not accepted.

Emotional Intelligence Gives Room For Initiatives And Inventions;

When all team members are aligned, it gives room for creativity, causing innovations.

IMPROVING EMOTIONAL INTELLIGENCE

Emotional Intelligence fuels your performance both in the working environment and in your life. Turning out to be genuinely cognizant permits us to develop and comprehend who we are, empowering us to discuss better with others and construct a more grounded relationship.

Unlike IQ, You can improve your emotional intelligence. Here are some steps and actions that can help you.

BE AN OPTIMIST

To stay motivated, it is of the utmost importance to keep an optimistic and positive mindset. See setbacks as an opportunity, also surround yourself with like minds.

LIFELONG LEARNING

As they say, learning never stops. Knowledge is what keeps us in trend with our environment. Make it a propensity to gain some new useful understanding. In this consistently changing universe of today, there's continually something to learn.

MONITOR YOUR FEELINGS

The days are filled with busy activities that we lose touch with our emotions. To reconnect, we need to pause and check how we feel emotionally and where it affects us physically.

CHECK HOW YOU REACT

It is good to know how you behave when some emotions are triggered in you or others.

TAKE RESPONSIBILITY

Since you are in control and no one else, it is good to accept how you behave or have behaved.

CELEBRATE POSITIVITY

Reflecting on negative feelings helps to understand and become a full person. It also helps in dealing with future occurrences.

GET CONFIDENT;

Think back on how you dealt with an issue in the past. This gives you the confidence that is needed for the present and the future.

BE HAPPY AND TAKE ACTION

You have goals set, be excited about them, and take necessary actions in reaching the goal.

MAKE ADJUSTMENT

Being conciliatory to your feelings makes you more aware of other people's emotions and birthing a good and healthy relationship.

- Don't be quick to judge without getting the facts right.
- Don't seek attention for your accomplishment. Give room for others to shine. Practice the attitude of humility.

GET FEEDBACK

Review your self-perception by asking colleagues, friends, and family how they would rate your emotional intelligence. For example, ask how you respond to difficult issues under pressure or how you handle conflicts.

READING

Readers are leaders. Reading helps with acquiring an understanding of others' viewpoints. That is, what makes them thick or how they respond to challenges faced.

PRACTICE RESPONSE, NOT REACTION

Reacting is a cognizant cycle that sees how you feel; however, choosing how you need to carry on. At the same time, responding is an unconscious process where we undergo emotional set-off and act rashly to ease the mood.

TAKE BREATHING EXERCISES

There are times we are hit by challenging situations that trigger emotions. This is the time to pause and breathe, then take a moment to avoid an outburst.

KEEP A JOURNAL

When things seem overwhelming, pick your diary and write out how you are feeling. With time, you feel lighter and better.

TAKE A BREAK

We are too occupied with activities that we forget to live, thereby causing an emotional breakdown. Take a break, travel, or do yoga.

HAVE A SCHEDULE

This is effective when you have a task to complete. It breaks the power of procrastination hard.

TRUST YOUR INSTINCTS

At the point when you appear to be uncertain about what to do, trust your impulses as your subliminal quality has realized which way to take.

BREAK FROM NORMS

One way to keep emotions in check is your sensory input. So, break out from the routine. Do or try something new.

GET OUT OF THERE

When a situation arises, and you feel you can't handle it, it is time to exit.

SEEK HELP

Whether you are a team lead or working with others on a project, attempt to stay open and receptive.

SET PERSONAL GOALS

Setting goal is enough to motivate.

BE APPROACHABLE

Whether you are a team leader or working on a project with others, try to remain accessible and approachable.

EAT WELL

A hungry man is an angry man. When you eat well, the right chemicals that trigger emotions are released.

DO NOT EXPECT TOO MUCH

The less you expect from people, the less hurt you will be when they don't meet your expectations. Make excuses for people. Avoid the drama of dwelling in the past, complaining, and selfishness.

PUT YOURSELF IN SOMEONE ELSE'S SHOES

Not literally, but imagine how you will feel or react if the same attitude is done to you.

ACTIONS ARE LOUDER THAN WORDS

Let your words commensurate with your actions. Your words might say something, but your body is telling another story.

Start making heroes of people who help others. It is not just the person that got to the top, but all the people who made it possible. This encourages good behavior.

EMOTIONAL INTELLIGENCE VERSUS COGNITIVE INTELLIGENCE - EQ VS. IQ

Over time, there have been various discussions and arguments on cognitive intelligence (IQ) and Emotional intelligence (EQ).

Therefore, we are going to be discussing the variance between EQ and IQ in the table below.

EMOTIONAL INTELLIGENCE	COGNITIVE INTELLIGENCE
Individuals with high EQ can distinguish, assess, control, and express feelings. They perceive and assess others' emotions, and they use emotions to facilitate thinking. They understand Emotional meaning.	They can learn, comprehend and apply information to abilities, have legitimate thinking, word cognizance, math abilities, unique and spatial reasoning, and superfluous channel data.
In their work environment, they are team players. They have leadership skills, successful relations, service orientation, and initiative collaboration.	They are successful with challenging tasks. They can associate specks, examination, and improvement.
They can recognize leaders, team players, people who best work alone, and those with social difficulties.	They can pick out exceptionally fit or skilled people or people with mental difficulties and uncommon necessities.

Emotional intelligence Is learned and improved with time.	Working memory holds data to manipulate it, while transient memory stores data for a brief timeframe. Examples, remembering details from a book read a few days ago and tuning in to a grouping of occasions in a story while attempting to comprehend the issue here.
Ensures success in life	It is an inborn ability.
In the business world, it plays a vital role in sales success. For example, a sales agent with initiative and self-confidence trickles in profits.	Ensures academic success

EQ is a proportion of a person's emotional intelligence level, which differentiated between various sentiments and utilized this insight to manage thinking and conduct. Simultaneously, IQ is the proportion of a person's insight level, which is reflected in the score got by the individual in the knowledge contrasted with the scores obtained by others of a similar age.

People with high IQs have fluid thinking. Fluid thinking is the capacity to think deftly and tackle issues.

They likewise have "information on the world. " That is, they have a comprehension of various subjects and teaches and how they identify with each other.

Example: ability to solve puzzles and come up with a problem-solving system. However, fluid reasoning tends to decline later in life.

Emotional intelligence is the "ability to reason with emotions validly and use emotions to enhance thought, while intelligence Quotient is a number derived from a standardized intelligence test.

Intelligence Quotient is scored by dividing an individual mental age by their chronological age and multiplying 100. (M÷C×100=IQ)

For example, a child's mental age is 12 and chronological age is 16, such a child will have an IQ of 75.

In conclusion, one's intelligence quotient determines one's competencies and individual capabilities. Still, emotional intelligence determines how we interact and treat people in our lives.

FEATURES OF A HIGH EMOTIONAL INTELLIGENCE PERSON

According to studies, it is found that higher emotional intelligence is positively associated with the following;

- Better social relations in children. Children with high EQ match up with good social interactions both in school and out of school.
- Adults with high EQ connect better with self-perception, thereby creating less interpersonal aggression or problems.
- Others perceive people with high EQ to be pleasant, socially skilled, and emphatic. In other words, a perfect being.

- People with high EQ tend to have greater achievement in academics. They are also believed to have higher life satisfaction, self-esteem, and lower levels of depression and insecurity.

As we have both high and low **IQ**, so do we have them in emotional intelligence.

What Is Low Emotional Intelligence?

Individuals with low **EQ** cannot understand why they feel how they do, think, and act the way they do. They have no grasp over their emotions and that of other people.

Below are ways to know if you are struggling with low **EQ**;

SIGNS OF LOW EMOTIONAL INTELLIGENCE

Poor At Reading People

When you start reading what people say beyond their words, it saves you from trouble and helps you respond effectively. On the other hand, misreading people can lead to problems as well. For example, if your friend seems lost and not paying attention, you begin to hold grudges or distance yourself from them, it shows you are poor at reading people, and your **EQ** is low.

They Are Always Right

Thinking you are always right or can't be corrected is a sign of low **EQ**. For instance, you get into an argument with people, turn a deaf ear to what people have to say, and feel offended when someone holds an opinion different from yours.

It is challenging to spend time with people because they live with regimented mindsets and are not ready to learn what they don't know due to their ego.

They fix People Emotions

When you try to fix other people's feelings of distress and vulnerability without validating them, it shows your **EQ** is low.

For example, a friend shares an ongoing issue in her life, rather than acknowledging her emotions by saying words like;

- I might not understand what you are going through, but you can always count on me,

- I have your back

You instead tell her why she shouldn't feel that way or ask her to snap out of the emotion.

Low or Non-Management of Emotions;

Recognizing and understanding your emotions is not enough but being able to manage them effectively. When you have a clear understanding of your emotional state, you tend to settle for the best choices concerning the circumstance.

A person with low Emotional intelligence fails to recognize their body and mind needs, thereby losing their temper and making things worse. On the other hand, an Emotionally intelligent person takes a day off from activities when feeling stressed out until he feels better.

Poor Coping Skills

You know a lot about a person's EQ level by how they act, especially during difficult conversations. Rather than cool things down and focus on **"agree to disagree,"** they make things worse.

Lack Of Empathy

The emotionally intelligent person is gifted in recognizing emotions, utilizing emotions, understanding emotions, and managing emotions.

Empathy permits you to detect others' emotions. For instance, you tell a mean or insensitive joke about a colleague, and people around you do not find it funny. Before you say something, learn to pause before judging, assuming, or reacting to anything or anyone.

Emotional Intelligence is a skill we all need to possess, and it takes time and practice to be perfected. Emotions are a fundamental wellspring of data for learning.

They Do Not Take Responsibility

A person with low **EQ** is never accountable for their words or actions. Their first reason for a response when something turns out badly is to shift the fault to another person. For instance, they go through your journal or diary without your consent and still find a way of blaming you when you call them out.

They Are Poor In Relationship Management

People with low **EQ** tend to come off as unfeeling and abrasive.

They don't have close companions since friendship requires a shared give and take, and they don't have the limit.

[202]

THE DARK SIDE OF EMOTIONAL INTELLIGENCE

As widely accepted and proclaimed, Emotional Intelligence is regarded as an essential skill to possess.

The usefulness of high emotional intelligence cannot be overemphasized. It is seen as one of the critical factors that can be effective listeners, communicators, and better decision-makers if anyone gets it.

Despite all these, arguments are going around about the side effects of emotional intelligence. In simple terms, high EQ can be used for good and evil.

Here are a few drawbacks of Emotional Intelligence:

WHAT IS THE DARK SIDE OF EMOTIONAL INTELLIGENCE?

Manipulation/Ability To Control Others

When you are aware of the other person's feelings, it is easy to motivate or encourage them to act against their interests. For instance, when we watch a profoundly emotional movie, we hardly check out the content. Another example is the message of Martin Luther king;

"America has given the Negro people a bad check."

"On the red hills of Georgia, sons of former slaves and the sons of former slave-owner will be able to sit down together at the table of brotherhood."

Such a message will arouse the consciousness of the hearer to wake up and do something.

Over- Promise and Under- deliver

The high EQ persons can create or paint appealing pictures of what it would be like when you take their advice. They can quickly wrap what is going on by fabricating lies, so it's challenging to know the facts from fiction.

Sizzling Impassioned Relationship

People with high Emotional intelligence are aware of and know the right people. However, they are usually superficial and habitually nosedive when push comes to shove.

Avoidance Of A Face-Off Or Evasion

On the one hand, high EQ helps to know how to pass on information without hurting others' feelings. On the other hand, high emotional intelligence serves as a means of Evasion.

For example, an elapsed deadline, a person with a high EQ won't be able to call such a person out. They are so aware of others that they shy away from correcting negative behaviors. While this is understandable, it becomes a challenge at the senior level as the responsibility of growth is left on one person.

Unreal, Fake or Excess Empathy

People with high EQ are better equipped to understand how others feel. Their empathy can be taken overboard or personal. Imagine how this might prevent team members from performing to their best ability in a busy working environment.

Gullibility

Studies have proven that people with high emotional intelligence are more vulnerable to empathic responses to issues where they are duped. For example, they easily fall prey to those who just want to use them for selfish purposes due to their high empathy level.

Repugnance for Risk

Most imaginative organizations require harmony between risk-taking and risk aversion. Individuals with high EQ will probably avoid any or all risks and maintain a strategic distance from intense decisions.

No Or Low Level Of Creativity And Innovative Potentials

High EQ characters will, in general, be great at following conventions, cooperating with other people yet come up short on the fundamental degrees of dereliction. It still comes down to risk aversion and reluctance to embrace change.

The outcomes recommend that having high EQ doesn't mean individuals will act with consideration with tests conducted. High social abilities don't make one pro-social.

Emotional skills are essential for a riddle yet are not all riddles. These abilities are invaluable. However, like any abilities, they will be used just if combined with other types of knowledge.

CONCLUSION

The Effect of Emotional Intelligence and Personal Relationships

As we looked into EQ's consequences on personal relationships and workplace performance, we have analyzed how emotional intelligence can impact these regions and the ethical implications of doing this. Since a sizable facet of emotional intelligence, as a complete, is related to the regulation of different people's feelings, the moral and ethical concerns raised by this procedure has to be considered.

Similarly, if you're a company owner or manager and are thinking about using EQ to train workers, assess potential advertising. So on, it's again essential to challenge your rights and duties in doing this.

-- *Happiness Factory*

THANK YOU FOR PURCHASING THIS MASTERPIECE FOR THE UNDERSTANDING THE ANXIETY FACED BY THE 20TH CENTURY COUPLES ALL OVER THE WORLD

Happiness Factory Book Series is dedicated to helping you sort out the problems that you face during your relationship. We have a dedicated team of researchers, writers, and editors who work tirelessly to provide the general people with the best information. We understand that you might be facing problems in the relationship, and the overly anxious behavior may be problematic for you. We will help you solve them and help you stay out of the dark.

We offer reliable and accurate information that is useful for both men and women. People of all ages can help from this book and help them retain the spark in their personal lives.

We look forward to seeing your comments that will help us provide an even better experience for you in the future.

HAPPINESS FACTORY
Be Who you Want!

CPSIA information can be obtained
at www.ICGtesting.com
Printed in the USA
BVHW041413220621
610211BV00005B/1633

9 781802 110586